Intermediate 2

# Biology

Specimen Question Paper

2000

2001

2002

2003



First exam published in 1999.

Published by

Leckie & Leckie, 8 Whitehill Terrace, St. Andrews, Scotland KY16 8RN

tel: 01334 475656 fax: 01334 477392

enquiries@leckieandleckie.co.uk www.leckieandleckie.co.uk

Leckie & Leckie Project Team: Peter Dennis; John MacPherson; Bruce Ryan; Andrea Smith

ISBN 1-84372-110-4

A CIP Catalogue record for this book is available from the British Library.

Printed in Scotland by Scotprint.

Leckie & Leckie is a division of Granada Learning Limited, part of Granada plc.

Leckie & Leckie

Scotland's leading educational publishers

# Introduction

Dear Student,

This past paper book provides you with the perfect opportunity to put into practice everything you need to know in order to excel in your exams. The range of past papers offers you an invaluable insight into what to expect on the day and will help you to prepare thoroughly for your own exam this summer.

Work carefully through each past paper: the questions are designed to assess not only your subject knowledge and understanding, but also your ability to apply examinable skills developed throughout your course. By referring to the answer booklet at the back of the book you will understand exactly what the examiner is looking for to gain a top mark and will be able to focus on and improve in particular areas of your course which you find difficult. Remember too to use the top tips for revision and sitting the exam to make sure you perform to the best of your ability.

Practice makes perfect. Use these past papers to make sure you know what to expect on the day and are ready to succeed.

Good luck!

# Acknowledgements

Every effort has been made to trace the copyright holders and to obtain their permission for the use of copyright material.
Leckie & Leckie will gladly receive information enabling them to rectify any error or omission in subsequent editions.

# INTERMEDIATE 2 SQP

FOR OFFICIAL USE

| Centre No. | Subject No. | Level | Paper No. | Group No. | Marker's No. |
|---|---|---|---|---|---|
| | 0300 | | | | |

Total

[C007/SQP042]

# Intermediate 2 Biology

Specimen Question Paper

Time: 2 hours

NATIONAL QUALIFICATIONS

**Fill in these boxes and read what is printed below.**

Full name of centre

Town

First name and initials

Surname

Date of birth
Day Month Year

Candidate number

Number of seat

**SECTION A (25 marks)**

Instructions for completion of Section A are given on page two.

**SECTIONS B AND C (75 marks)**

1 (a) All questions should be attempted.

(b) It should be noted that in **Section C** questions 1 and 2 each contain a choice.

2 The questions may be answered in any order but all answers are to be written in the spaces provided in this answer book, and must be written clearly and legibly in ink.

3 Additional space for answers and rough work will be found at the end of the book. If further space is required, supplementary sheets may be obtained from the invigilator and should be inserted inside the front cover of this book.

4 The numbers of questions must be clearly inserted with any answers written in the additional space.

5 Rough work, if any should be necessary, should be written in this book and then scored through when the fair copy has been written.

6 Before leaving the examination room you must give this book to the invigilator. If you do not, you may lose all the marks for this paper.

**Read carefully**

1 Check that the answer sheet provided is for Intermediate 2 Biology (Section A).

2 Fill in the details required on the answer sheet.

3 In this paper a question is answered by indicating the choice A, B, C or D by a stroke made in **ink** in the appropriate place in the answer sheet—see the sample question below.

4 For each question there is only **one** correct answer.

5 Rough working, if required, should be done only on this question paper—or on the rough working sheet provided—**not** on the answer sheet.

6 At the end of the examination the answer sheet for Section A **must not** be placed inside the answer book, but should be handed separately to the invigilator.

**Sample Question**

Which of the following are the raw materials for photosynthesis?

A Carbon dioxide and glucose

B Carbon dioxide and water

C Oxygen and water

D Oxygen and glucose

The correct answer is **B**—carbon dioxide and water. A **heavy** vertical line should be drawn joining the two dots in the appropriate box in the column headed **B** as shown in the example on the answer sheet.

If, after you have recorded your answer, you decide that you have made an error and wish to make a change, you should cancel the original answer and put a vertical stroke in the box you now consider to be correct. Thus, if you want to change an answer D to an answer B, your answer sheet would look like this:

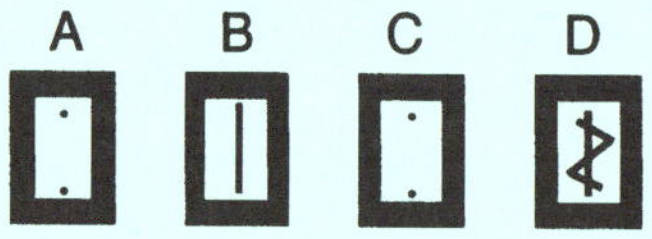


If you want to change back to an answer which has already been scored out, you should enter a tick (✓) to the **right** of the box of your choice, thus:

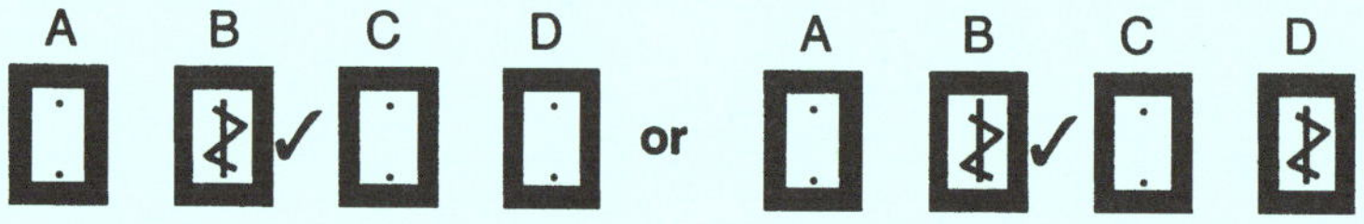

## SECTION A

**All questions in this section should be attempted.**

**Answers should be given on the separate answer sheet provided.**

**1.** Which of the following can be used to describe yeast?

A Animal

B Bacterium

C Macrophage

D Fungus

**2.** Which of the following is only found in plant cells?

A Cell membrane

B Nucleus

C Cytoplasm

D Cell wall

**3.** In an investigation into the digestion of a protein food, the time taken for a cube of protein to be digested was recorded. Four samples were used.

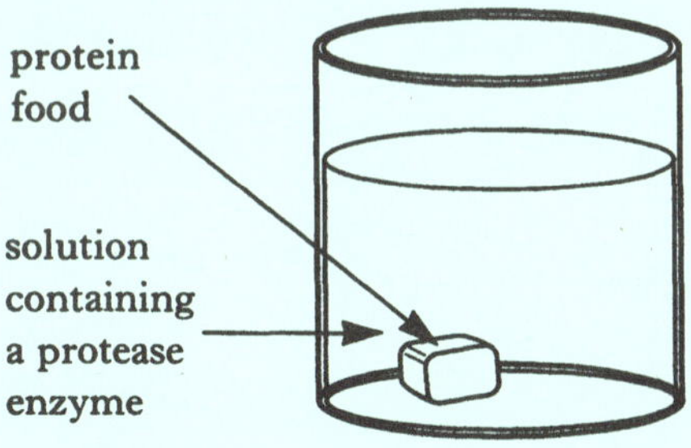


The results are recorded in the table below.

| *Protein food* | *Time taken for complete digestion* |
|---|---|
| sample 1 | 6 hours 50 minutes |
| sample 2 | 6 hours 40 minutes |
| sample 3 | 7 hours |
| sample 4 | 7 hours 10 minutes |

The average time taken to digest the protein was

A 7 hours 25 minutes

B 6 hours 55 minutes

C 6·55 hours

D 6·85 minutes.

**4.** Which of the following graphs best shows the effect of temperature on the activity of an enzyme?

A

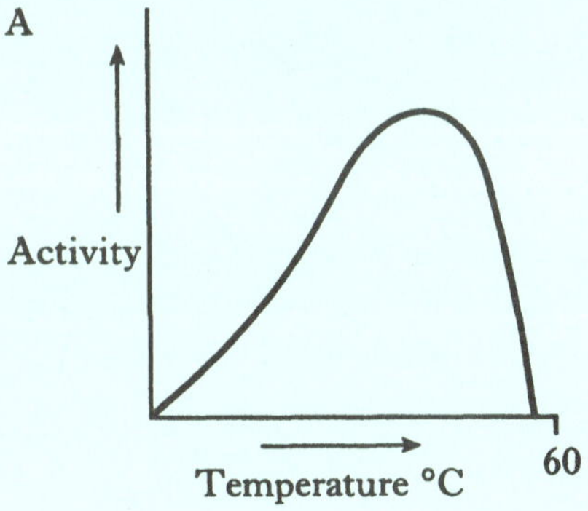


B

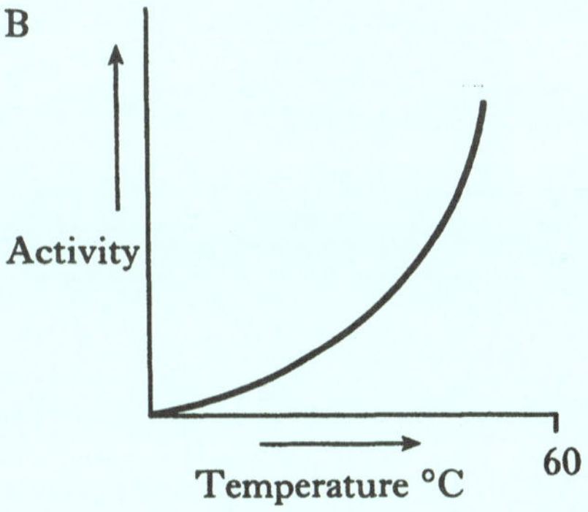


C

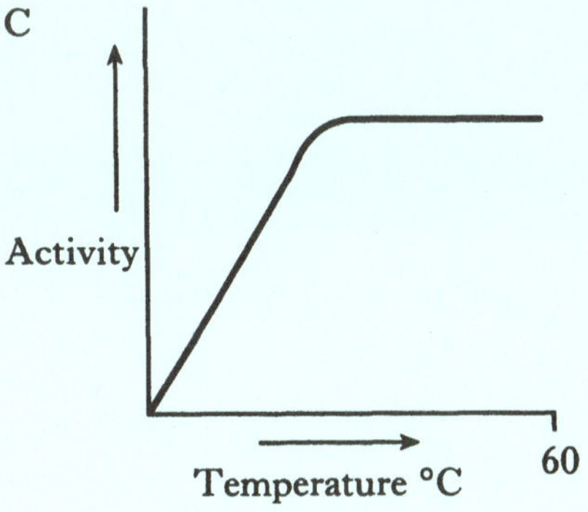


D

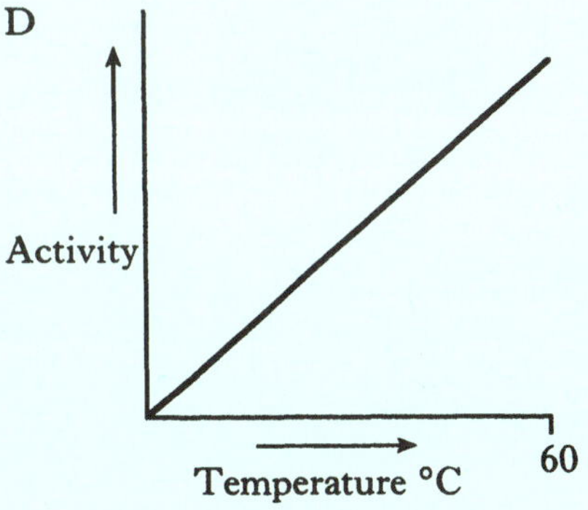

**5.** The diagram below shows part of an investigation, carried out by a student, into the action of the enzyme amylase.

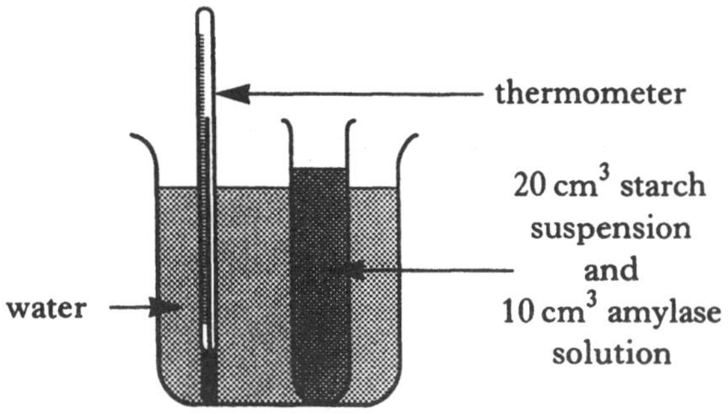


At the end of the investigation, the student concluded that the amylase had broken down the starch into sugar.

Which of the following would be a suitable control for this investigation?

A

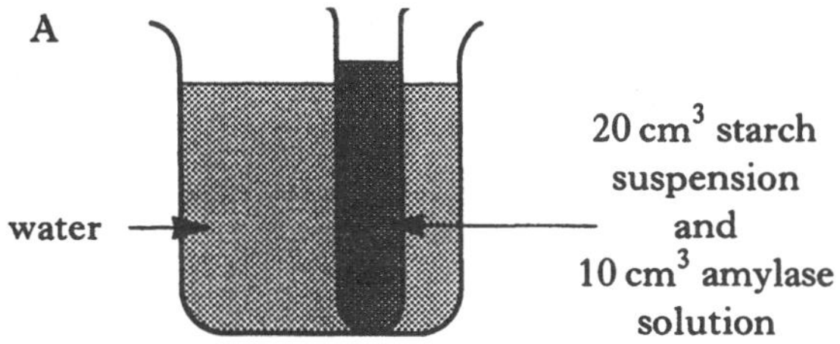


B

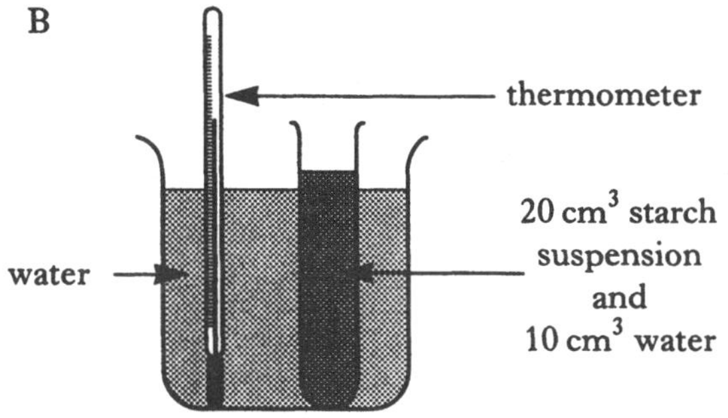


C

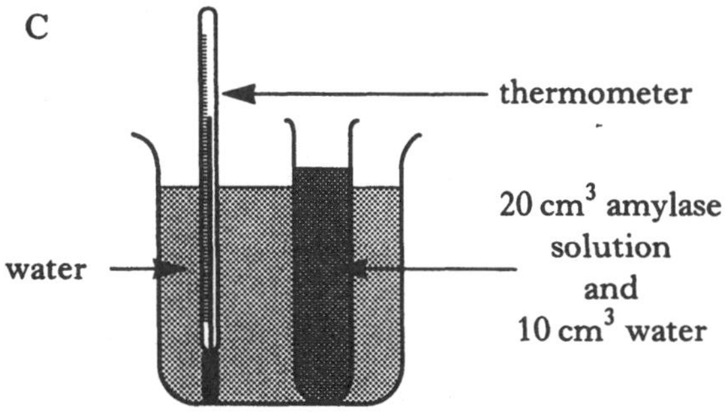


D

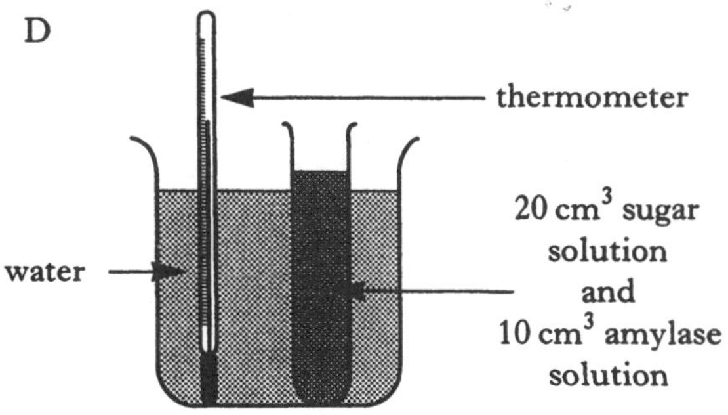


**6.** The graph shows the effect of light intensity, concentration of carbon dioxide and temperature on the rate of photosynthesis.

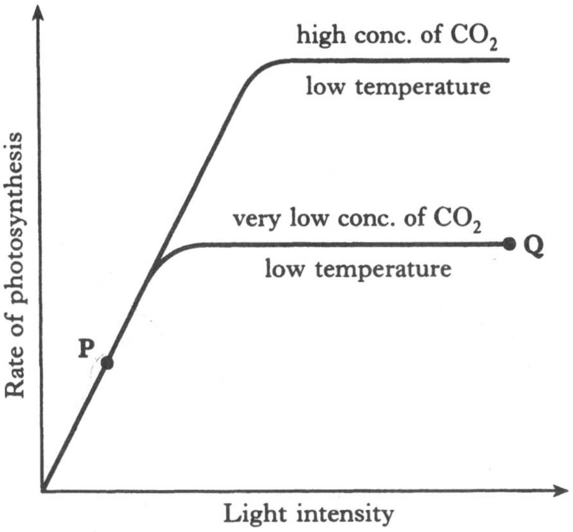


Which factors are limiting the rate of photosynthesis at points P and Q on the graph?

| | P | Q |
|---|---|---|
| A | light | carbon dioxide |
| B | light | temperature |
| C | carbon dioxide | temperature |
| D | temperature | light |

**Questions 7 and 8** refer to the graph below.

An investigation was carried out into the effect of increasing the concentration of carbon dioxide in the air on a person's breathing.

The graph below shows how increasing the percentage of carbon dioxide in the air affects the volume of air inhaled each minute.

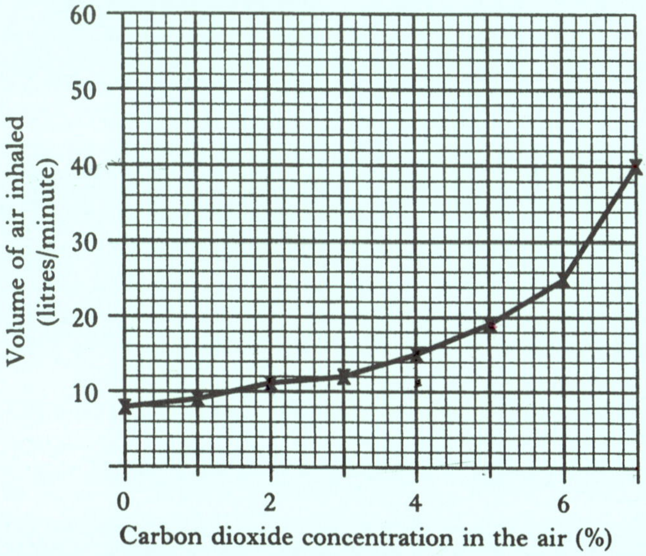


7. The volume of **carbon dioxide** entering the lungs each minute when the concentration of carbon dioxide in the air is 7%, is

   A 2·8 litres

   B 17·5 litres

   C 28·0 litres

   D 40·0 litres.

8. When the carbon dioxide concentration of the air is increased from 2% to 5%, the volume of air inhaled increases by

   A 6 litres/minute

   B 8 litres/minute

   C 10 litres/minute

   D 19 litres/minute.

9. Which of the following describes a community within an ecosystem?

   A All the animals

   B All the plants

   C All the plants and animals

   D The total number of one species

10. The diagram shows part of a food web in Californian scrubland.

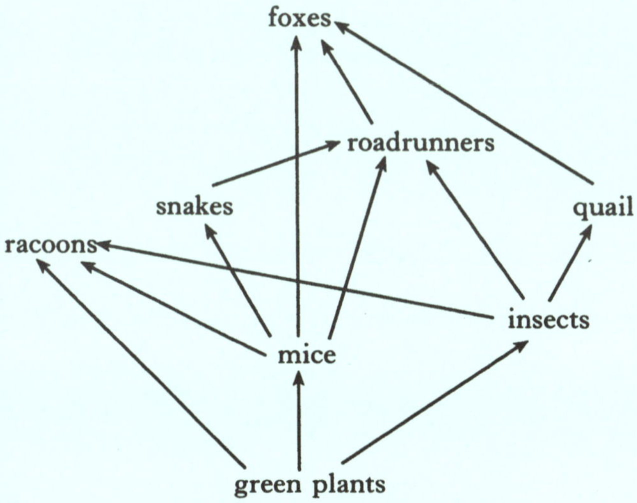


Which of the following organisms are in competition for mice?

   A Racoons and insects

   B Quail and racoons

   C Roadrunners and insects

   D Snakes and roadrunners

**Questions 11 and 12** refer to the information below.

| *Organism* | *Pairs of wings* | *Appearance of wings* | *Type of mouthparts* |
|---|---|---|---|
| Dog flea | 0 | – | sucking |
| Ladybird | 2 | hardened | biting |
| Aphid | 2 | transparent | sucking |
| Bird louse | 0 | – | biting |
| Butterfly | 2 | coloured | sucking |

**Key**

1. no wings .................................. go to 2
   two pairs of wings ..................... go to 3

2. ............................. Dog flea
   ............................. Bird louse

3. wings transparent ..................... Aphid
   wings not transparent ............... go to 4

4. ............................. Ladybird
   ............................. Butterfly

In the key above, two of the numbered pairs of statements have been omitted.

Answer the following **two** questions by selecting the correct pair of statements.

Pairs of statements

A no wings
two pairs of wings

B sucking mouthparts
biting mouthparts

C wings hardened
wings coloured

D one pair of wings
two pairs of wings

**11.** Which pair of statements fits into 2?

**12.** Which pair of statements fits into 4?

**13.** The process by which organisms that are better adapted to their environment survive and breed, while those less well adapted fail to do so, is called

A biodiversity

B environmental impact

C natural selection

D genetic engineering.

**14.** Different forms of a gene are called

A phenotypes

B alleles

C gametes

D genotypes.

**15.** The apparatus below was used to show that bacteria in soil respire and release carbon dioxide.

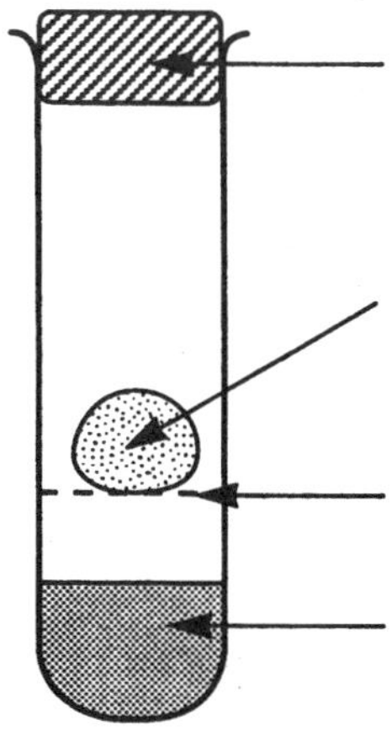


Which of the following would provide the most suitable control?

Apparatus as above, but

A no stopper

B no soil

C an equal mass of baked and cooled soil

D no indicator solution.

16. A salt water bony fish maintains the osmotic concentration of its body fluids by

A drinking water and eliminating salt from the gills

B drinking water and absorbing salts through the gills

C eliminating excess water as dilute urine

D absorbing water through the gills.

17. Some air-breathing mammals, such as certain species of seals, whales, and dolphins, have adaptations which enable them to make long underwater dives in search of food.

The table below shows the distribution of stored oxygen in a Weddell seal compared with a human.

| | *Total oxygen stored (%)* | | |
|---|---|---|---|
| | *In the lung capillaries* | *In muscles* | *In the rest of body* |
| Weddell seal | 5 | 26 | 69 |
| Human | 35 | 13 | 52 |

The ratio of oxygen stored in the lung capillaries of humans to that stored in the lung capillaries of Weddell seals is

A 7 : 1

B 2 : 1

C 1 : 7

D 1 : 2.

**Questions 18, 19 and 20** refer to the diagram of the human digestive system shown below.

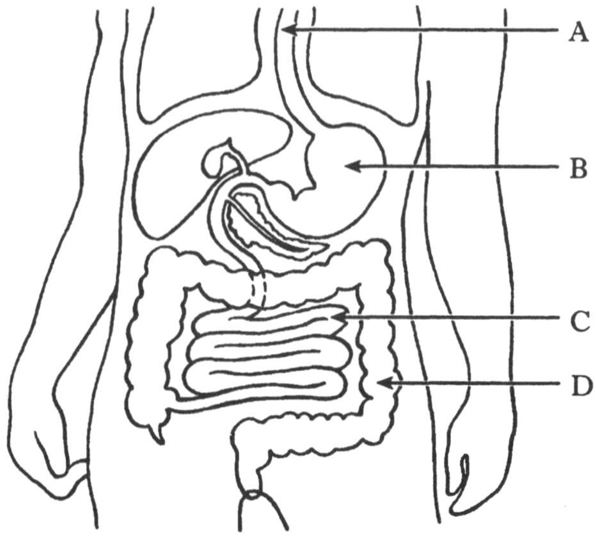


18. In which part are carbohydrates mainly absorbed?

19. In which part is water mainly absorbed?

20. Which labelled arrow is pointing to the stomach?

21. Solid food is passed along the gut by

A osmosis

B peristalsis

C digestion

D excretion.

22. Which part of the brain is involved in the control of heart rate?

A Cerebellum

B Cerebrum

C Medulla

D Hypothalamus

**23.** Which of the following pairs of corrective mechanisms would occur in response to an increase in body temperature?

A Dilation of blood capillaries in the skin
**and**
Increased activity of sweat glands

B Dilation of blood capillaries in the skin
**and**
Decreased activity of sweat glands

C Constriction of blood capillaries in the skin
**and**
Increased activity of sweat glands

D Constriction of blood capillaries in the skin
**and**
Decreased activity of sweat glands

**Questions 24 and 25** refer to the information below.

The table below shows the changes in the volume of blood circulating in a number of parts of the body before and during exercise.

| *Part of body* | *Volume of blood circulating ($cm^3$/minute)* | |
|---|---|---|
| | *Before exercise* | *During exercise* |
| Heart muscle | 300 | 900 |
| Muscles attached to the skeleton | 1200 | 12 000 |
| Skin | 600 | 1900 |
| Muscles of the gut | 1500 | 600 |

**24.** For heart muscles the blood flow during exercise increases by

A 3 times

B 4 times

C 10 times

D 30 times.

**25.** The change in the blood flow to the gut during exercise is a decrease of

A 40 %

B 50 %

C 60 %

D 67 %.

**Candidates are reminded that the answer sheet MUST NOT be returned inside this answer book.**

Candidates must not write in this margin

*Marks*

## SECTION B

**All questions in this section should be attempted.**

**1.** (*a*) The diagram below summarises photosynthesis.

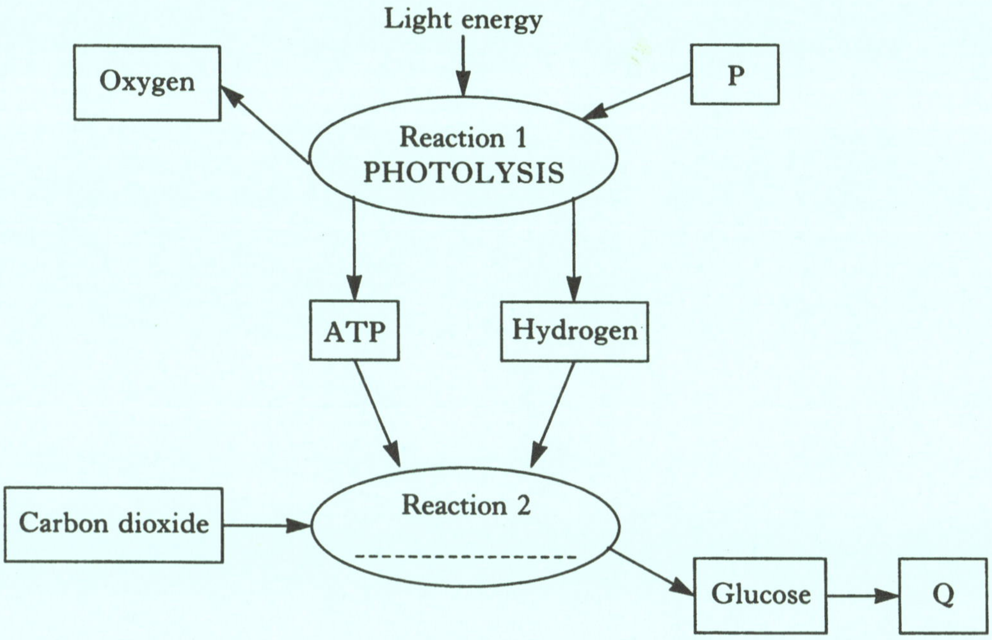


(i) Name the molecule which absorbs light energy.

________________________ **(1)**

(ii) Identify P, the source of the hydrogen produced by photolysis.

________________________ **(1)**

(iii) The energy conversion taking place in Reaction 1 is

light energy ——► ________________ energy. **(1)**

(iv) Reaction 1 is called photolysis.
What name is given to Reaction 2?

________________________ **(1)**

(v) Compound Q is a component of plant cell walls.
Identify Q.

________________________ **(1)**

Candidates must not write in this margin

Marks

**1. (continued)**

(*b*) The diagrams below show the movement of carbon dioxide between green leaves of a certain plant and the atmosphere in different light conditions over a 24 hour period.

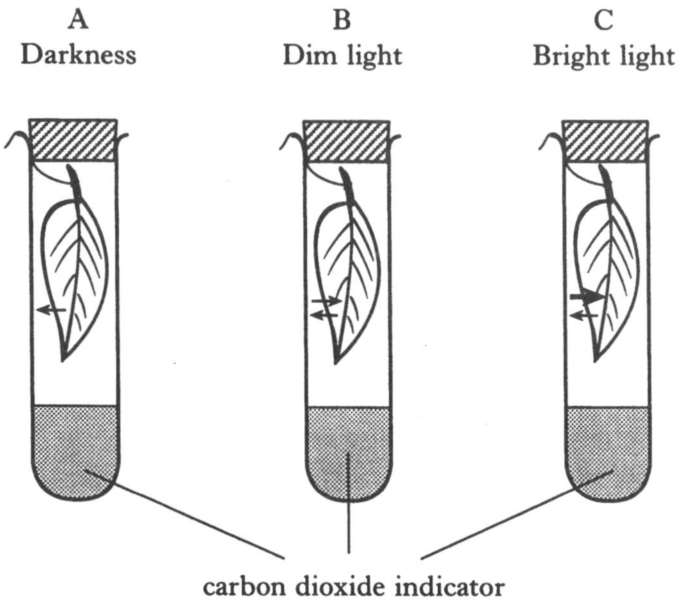


Each arrow represents the direction of carbon dioxide movement between the leaf and the atmosphere.

The thicker the arrow, the greater the volume of carbon dioxide moving.

The carbon dioxide indicator has the colour changes shown below.

Purple ← Red → Yellow

(air minus carbon dioxide) — (normal air) — (air plus carbon dioxide)

(i) Complete the table of results by writing the final colour of indicator in each container.

| *Container* | *Final colour of indicator* |
|---|---|
| A | |
| B | |
| C | |

**(2)**

*Marks*

**1. (*b*) continued**

(ii) Describe the **control tubes** which would be needed before a valid conclusion could be drawn.

________________________________________________

________________________________________________ **(1)**

(iii) Identify the containers in which (1) respiration and (2) photosynthesis was the dominant process.

(1) Respiration: Container ________

(2) Photosynthesis: Container ________ **(2)**

Candidates must not write in this margin

Marks

**2.** The diagram below shows part of a freshwater pond.

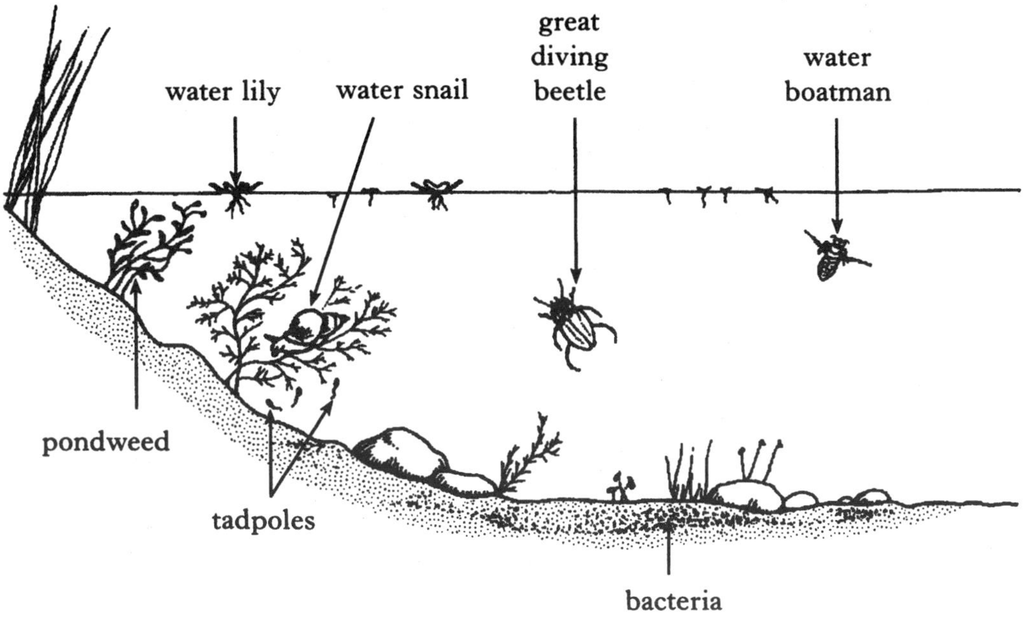


(*a*) (i) The table below contains information about organisms in the pond.

| *Organism(s)* | *Information* |
|---|---|
| Pondweed | Carries out photosynthesis |
| Water boatman | Attacks tadpoles and sucks their juices |
| Tadpole | Feeds on pondweed |
| Water snail | Feeds on pondweed |
| Great diving beetle | Kills and eats other insects |
| Bacteria | Feed on remains of other organisms |

Use this information to select examples to complete the table below.

| | *Example* |
|---|---|
| Primary consumer | |
| Predator | |
| Decomposer | |

**(3)**

*Marks*

**2. (*a*) (continued)**

(ii) Complete the food chain below, using information from the table.

[ ] → Tadpole → [ ] → [ ] **(1)**

(*b*) Explain what is meant by the term ***pyramid of biomass***.

________________________________________

________________________________________

________________________________________ **(2)**

Marks

3. An investigation on the effects of the presence of plants on soil erosion was carried out. The diagram below shows the apparatus used.

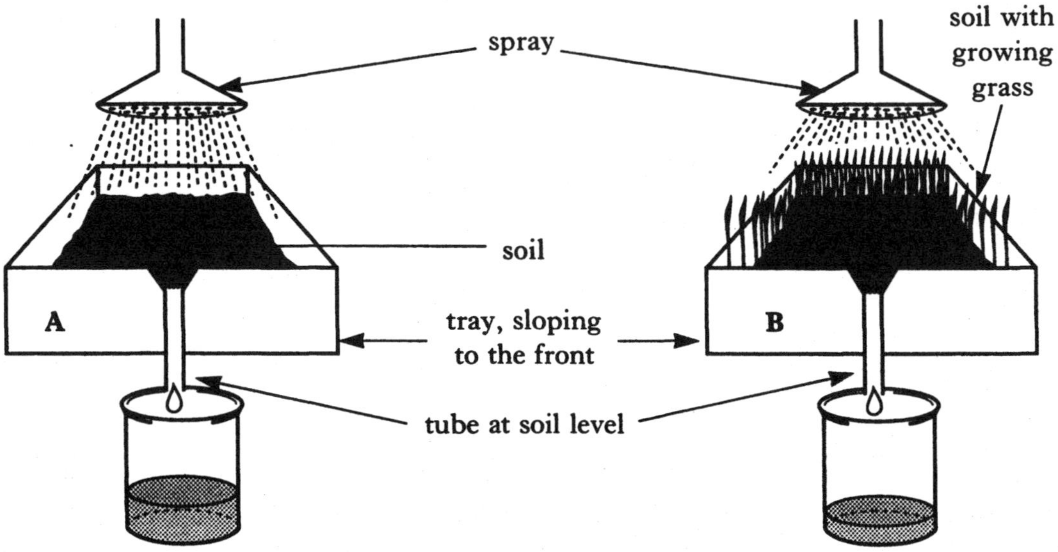


Tray **A** contained soil only.

Tray **B** contained the same type of soil but with grass growing on it.

Water from a spray was allowed to fall onto each tray. Any water running off was collected and examined for soil washed from the tray.

(*a*) Identify the variable which was altered in the investigation.

______________________________ **(1)**

(*b*) Describe **two** variables which must be kept constant in both sets of apparatus during the investigation.

1 ______________________________

2 ______________________________ **(2)**

(*c*) The investigation was set up to test the hypothesis that the presence of plants reduces soil erosion.
Suggest **one** measurement or observation required in order to confirm or reject the hypothesis.

______________________________

______________________________ **(1)**

Candidates must not write in this margin

*Marks*

4. The following diagram shows the production of sex cells in humans.

The numbers show the number of chromosomes in the cells.

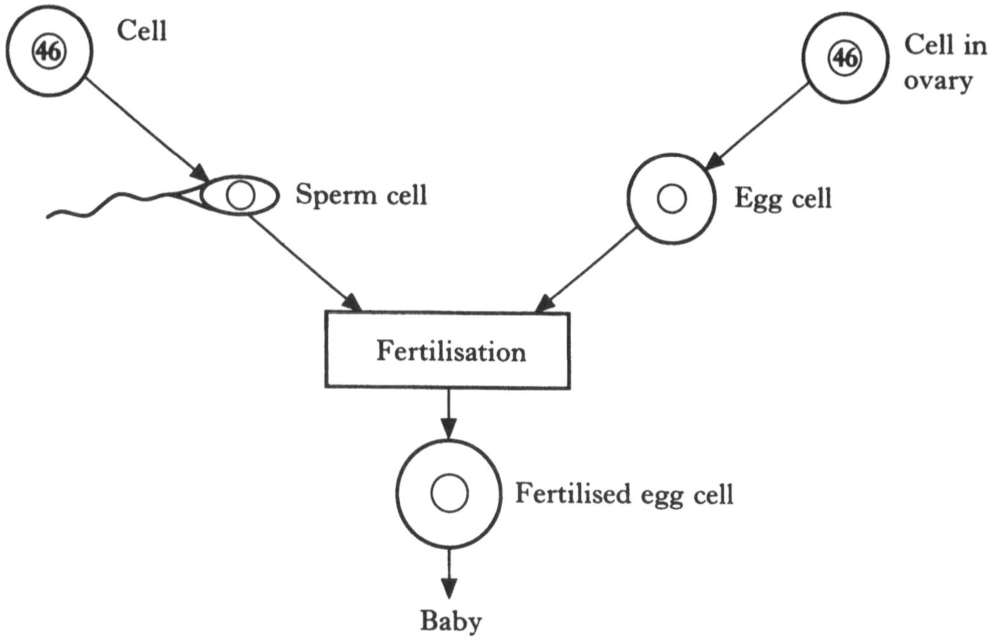


(*a*) Where are sperm produced?

________________________ **(1)**

(*b*) What is the term used for a fertilised egg cell?

________________________ **(1)**

(*c*) How many chromosomes are there in each egg cell?

________ **(1)**

(*d*) The baby is a girl.

Which of the sex-determining chromosomes did she inherit from her father?

________ **(1)**

Candidates must not write in this margin

*Marks*

5. (*a*) Blowflies lay eggs which hatch into larvae.

The following table shows the effect of light intensity on the speed of movement of blowfly larvae.

| *Light intensity (units)* | *Speed of movement (cm per minute)* |
|---|---|
| 0 | 1·6 |
| 20 | 3·6 |
| 40 | 3·8 |
| 60 | 4·0 |
| 80 | 4·6 |
| 90 | 5·1 |

(i) On the grid below, plot a suitable line graph to show the effects of increasing light intensity on the speed of movement of the blowfly larvae.

(Additional graph paper, if required, will be found on page 32.)

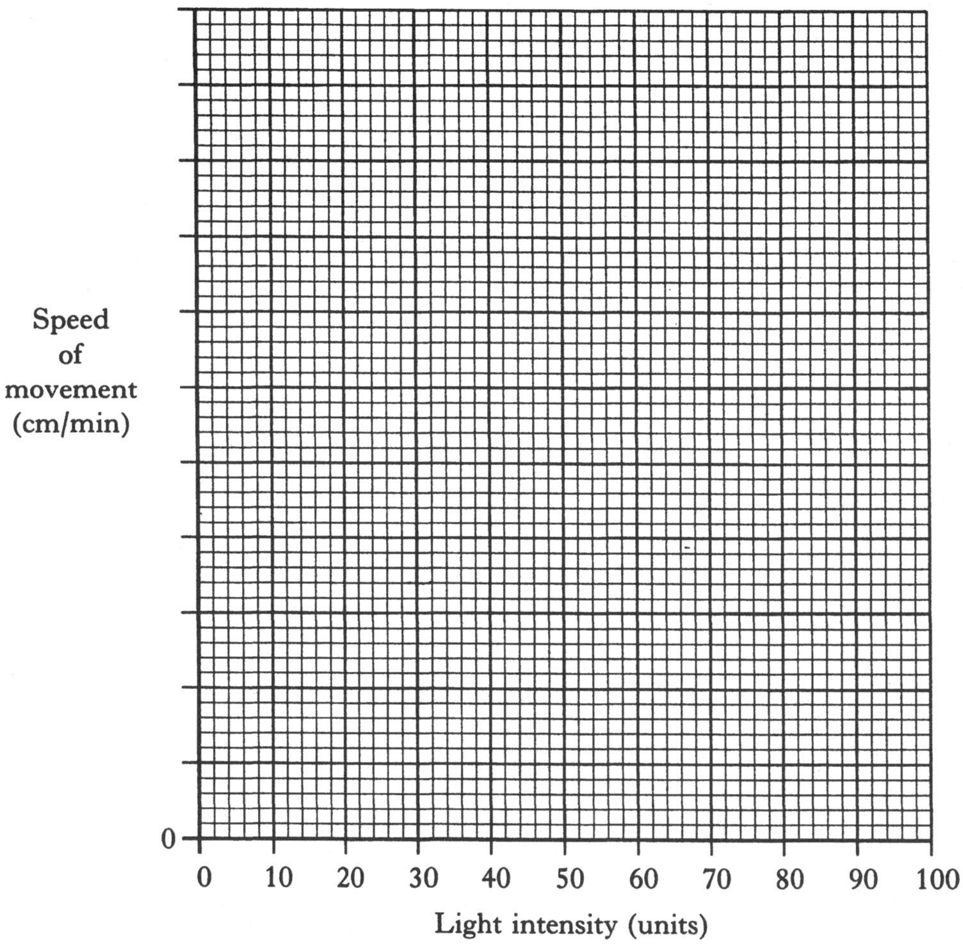


**(2)**

Candidates must not write in this margin

*Marks*

**5. (*a*) (continued)**

(ii) Describe the relationship between the intensity of the light and the speed of movement of the larvae.

________________________________________________

________________________________________________ **(1)**

(*b*) Some organisms, eg woodlice, move more rapidly in dry conditions than in damp conditions.

Explain how this contributes to their survival.

________________________________________________

________________________________________________

________________________________________________ **(2)**

Candidates must not write in this margin

*Marks*

6. True-breeding fruit flies with normal wings were crossed with true-breeding fruit flies which had vestigial wings. All the offspring had normal wings.

Two of these offspring, D and E, were crossed together and the next generation contained normal winged and vestigial winged flies.

Some of the flies in these crosses are shown in the diagram below.

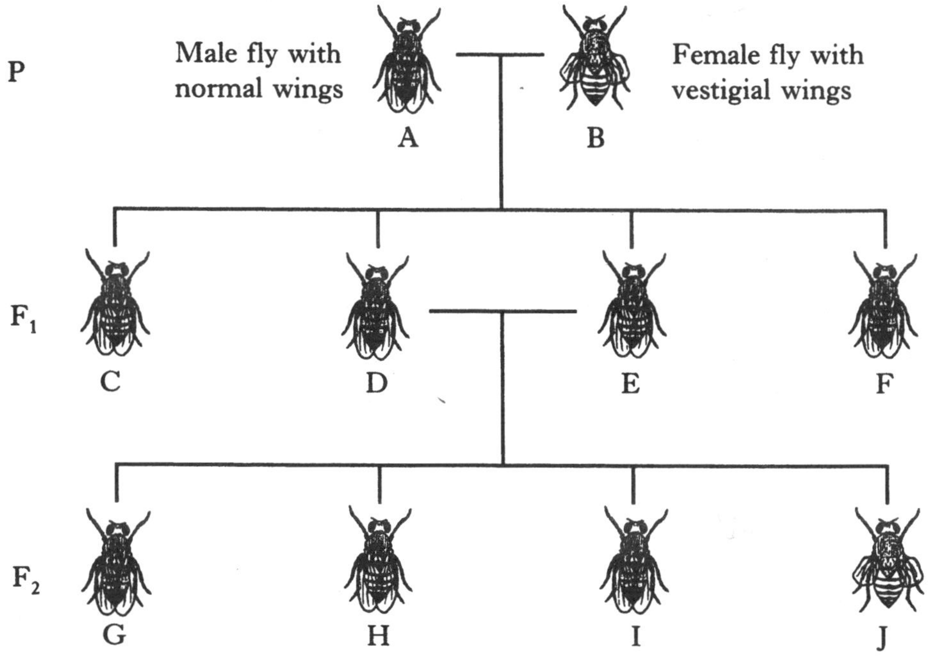


Use the letters from the diagram to answer the following questions.

(*a*) (i) Identify **two** flies from **different generations** which have the same phenotype.

Fly ________ and Fly ________

Describe that phenotype.

________________________________ **(1)**

(ii) State the dominant wing characteristic of the flies used in these crosses.

________________________________ **(1)**

(iii) From the parental and first generation only, identify **two** flies which have the same phenotype but different genotypes.

Fly ________ and Fly ________ **(1)**

Candidates must not write in this margin

*Marks*

**6. (continued)**

(*b*) In a second experiment ten $F_1$ flies were selected and bred together.

The $F_2$ generation of flies was examined and counted and the results are shown in the table below.

| | *Number of flies* |
|---|---|
| Flies with normal wings | 153 |
| Flies with vestigial wings | 39 |

(i) In a cross like this, what would be the expected number of flies with vestigial wings in the $F_2$ generation?

*Space for working*

________________ flies **(1)**

(ii) Give **one** reason to account for the difference between the expected number and actual number of flies with vestigial wings in the $F_2$ generation of this cross.

________________________________________

________________________________________ **(1)**

Candidates must not write in this margin

*Marks*

**7.** (*a*) Cellulase and pectinase are enzymes which break down different parts of plant cell walls. These enzymes are used in the commercial production of apple juice.

A group of students carried out an investigation into the effect of these enzymes on apple tissue at room temperature (20 °C).

The diagram below shows the apparatus used.

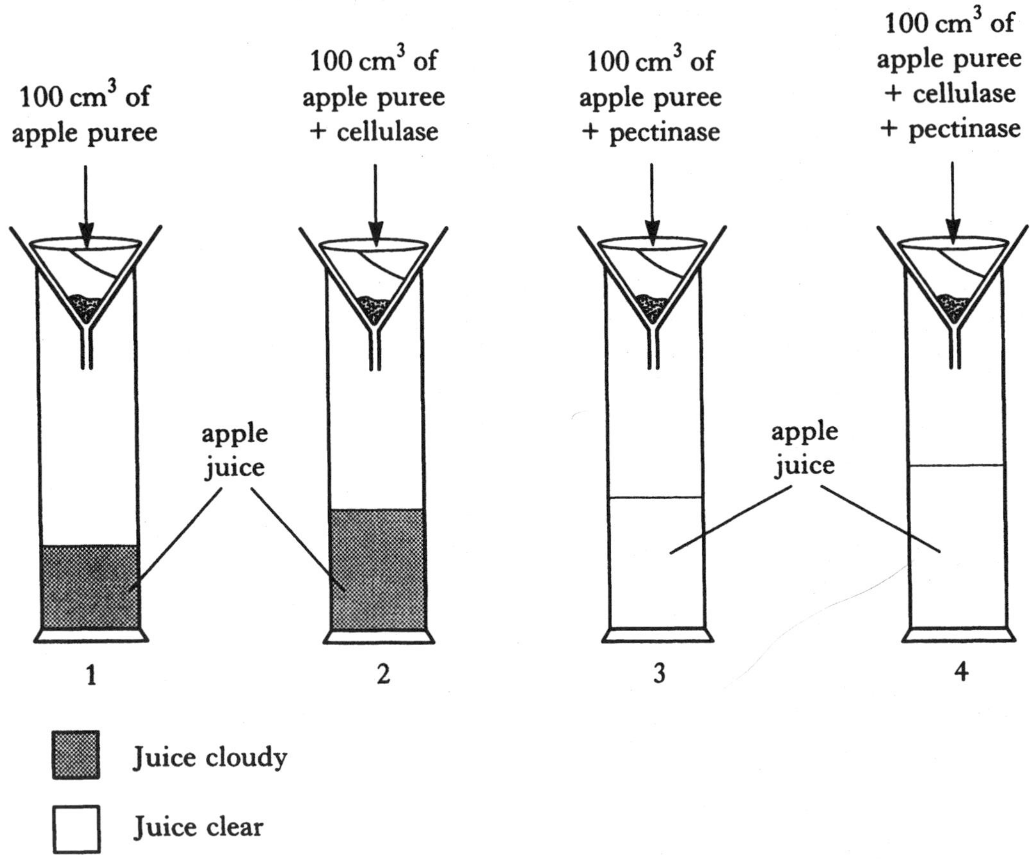


The investigation was left for 24 hours and then the volume of apple juice in each cylinder measured.

The results are shown in the table below.

| *Cylinder* | 1 | 2 | 3 | 4 |
|---|---|---|---|---|
| Volume of apple juice extracted ($cm^3$) | 25 | 34 | 39 | 50 |

Candidates must not write in this margin

*Marks*

**7. (a) (continued)**

(i) Calculate the volume of apple puree required to produce 1000 $cm^3$ of apple juice, if **both** enzymes were used in the extraction.

*Space for calculation*

______________________ **(1)**

(ii) Predict the effect on the volume of apple juice which would be extracted if the cylinders were placed in a refrigerator at 3 °C for the 24 hours, instead of being kept at room temperature.

______________________

______________________ **(1)**

(iii) State **one** effect of the addition of pectinase on the extraction of apple juice.

______________________ **(1)**

(*b*) The diagram below represents the molecular structure of cellulase – the enzyme which breaks down cellulose in plant cell walls.

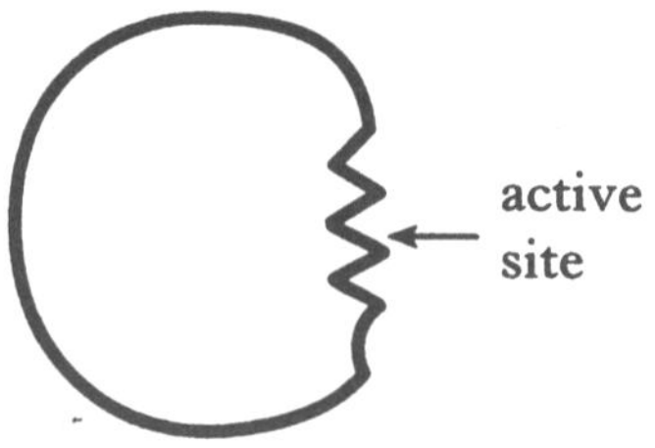


Use the information given above to explain the *specificity* of cellulase.

______________________

______________________ **(1)**

(*c*) Enzymes act as catalysts.
Describe **two** characteristics of catalysts.

1 ______________________

______________________

2 ______________________

______________________ **(2)**

Candidates must not write in this margin

*Marks*

**8.** The effect of pH on the activity of two protease enzymes, pepsin and trypsin, was investigated.

An enzyme solution, adjusted to the required pH, was placed in a hole made in the middle of a layer of gelatin in a petri dish. Gelatin is a jelly made of protein.

After one hour the activity of the enzymes was estimated by measuring the area of gelatin digested by the enzyme.

The results are shown in the graph below.

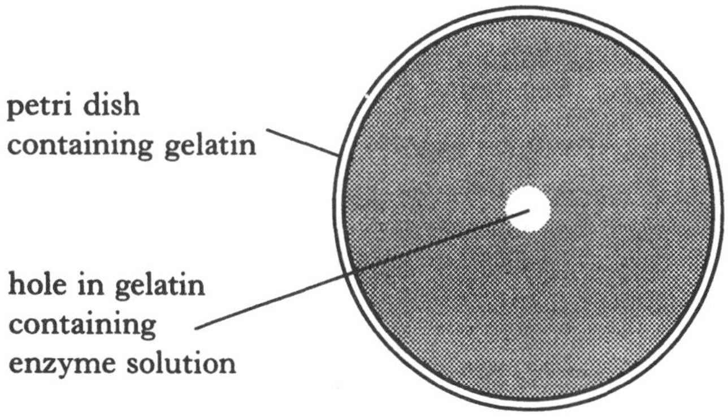


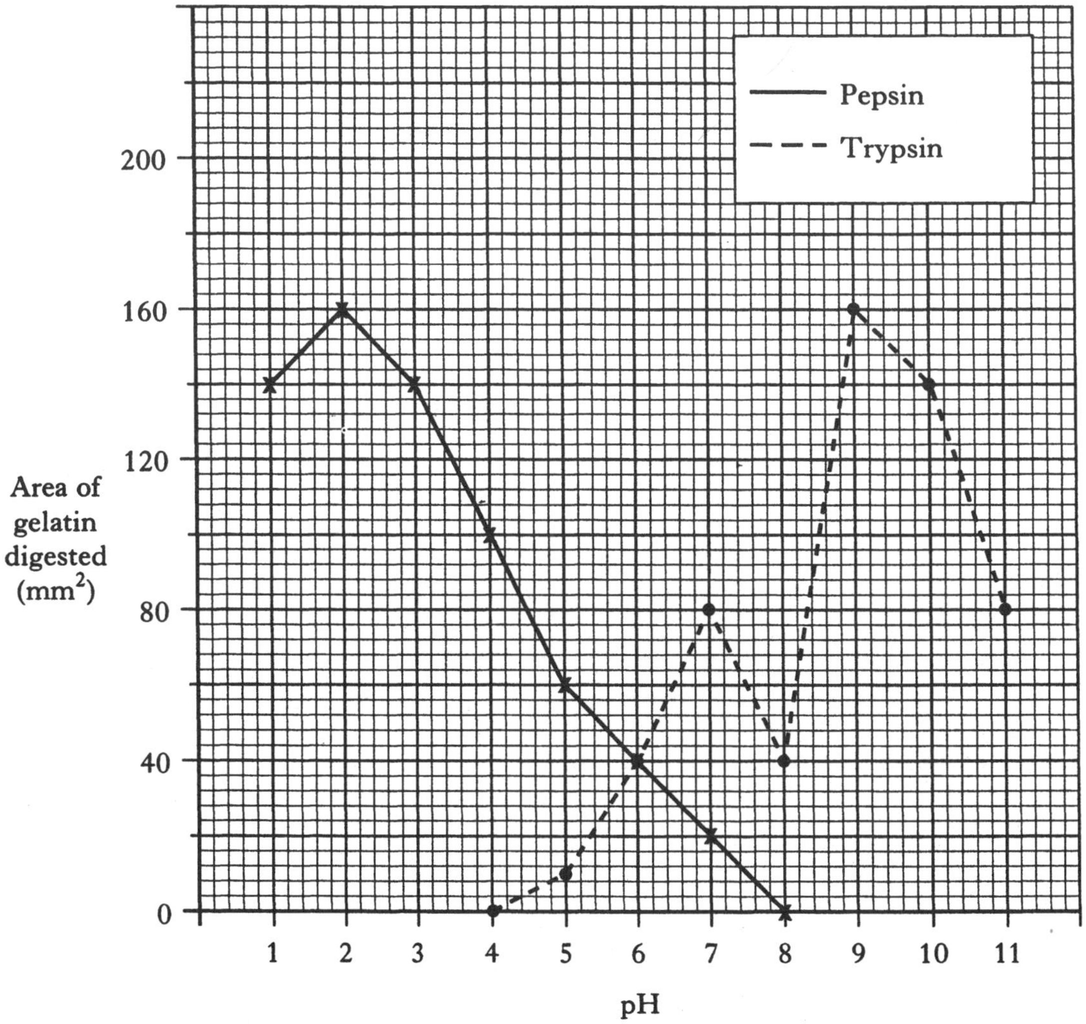

Candidates must not write in this margin

*Marks*

**8. (continued)**

(*a*) Identify the pH at which both enzymes were equally active.

__________ **(1)**

(*b*) The students suspected that one of the results may have been due to experimental error.

(i) Identify this result.

Enzyme ______________

pH ______________ **(1)**

(ii) Suggest a possible explanation for the experimental error.

________________________________________

________________________________________

________________________________________

________________________________________ **(1)**

(*c*) The optimum pH for pepsin is pH2.

This condition is found in the stomach.

Explain how this condition is created in the stomach.

________________________________________

________________________________________ **(1)**

Candidates must not write in this margin

*Marks*

**9.** The diagram below represents two responses of the human body to invasion by bacteria.

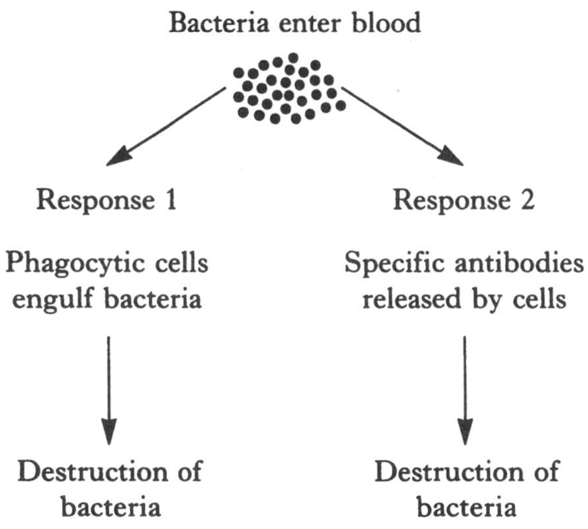


(*a*) Name a type of cell which carries out phagocytosis.

______________________________ **(1)**

(*b*) Name the type of cell which releases antibodies.

______________________________ **(1)**

(*c*) Explain what is meant by the term *specific* with reference to antibodies.

______________________________

______________________________

______________________________ **(1)**

Candidates must not write in this margin

*Marks*

**10.** In an investigation, the effect of drinking a litre of salty water was monitored by measuring the volume of urine excreted and its salt concentration every 30 minutes for 2 hours.

At 30 minutes, 55 $cm^3$ of urine with a salt concentration of 5 grams per litre was collected; at 60 minutes, 132 $cm^3$ of urine with a salt concentration of 14 grams per litre was collected; at 90 minutes, 210 $cm^3$ of urine with a salt concentration of 17 grams per litre was collected. At the end of the investigation, 112 $cm^3$ of urine with a salt concentration of 13 grams per litre was collected.

(*a*) Present this data in a table. **(2)**

(*b*) Describe what happens to the salt concentration of the urine as the investigation proceeds.

________________________________________ **(1)**

(*c*) The hormone ADH acts on the kidney tubules to control water balance.

Use the words **increases** or **decreases** in each space to complete the following paragraph correctly.

After a long period without drinking, the water concentration of the blood ________________. The production of ADH by the pituitary gland ________________ and the reabsorption of water by the kidney tubules ________________. As a result, the water concentration of the urine ________________. **(2)**

*Marks*

**11.** (*a*) The diagram below shows some of the structures in the human heart.

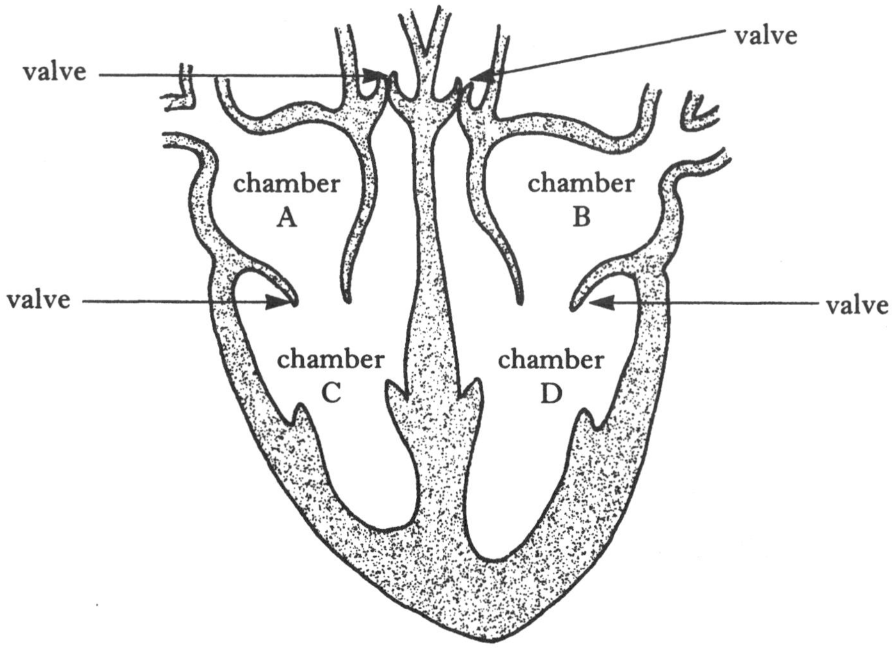


(i) **Underline** one word in each box to make the sentence correct.

| | | |
|---|---|---|
| Heart chamber A is the | right<br>left | ventricle<br>atrium |

**(1)**

(ii) **Draw arrows on the diagram** to show the direction of blood flow into and out of chamber B. **(1)**

(iii) Describe the function of the valves in the heart.

______________________________

______________________________ **(1)**

(iv) Explain why the wall of chamber D is thicker than the wall of chamber C.

______________________________

______________________________ **(1)**

Candidates must not write in this margin

*Marks*

**11. (continued)**

(*b*) The diagram below shows an exterior view of a human heart.

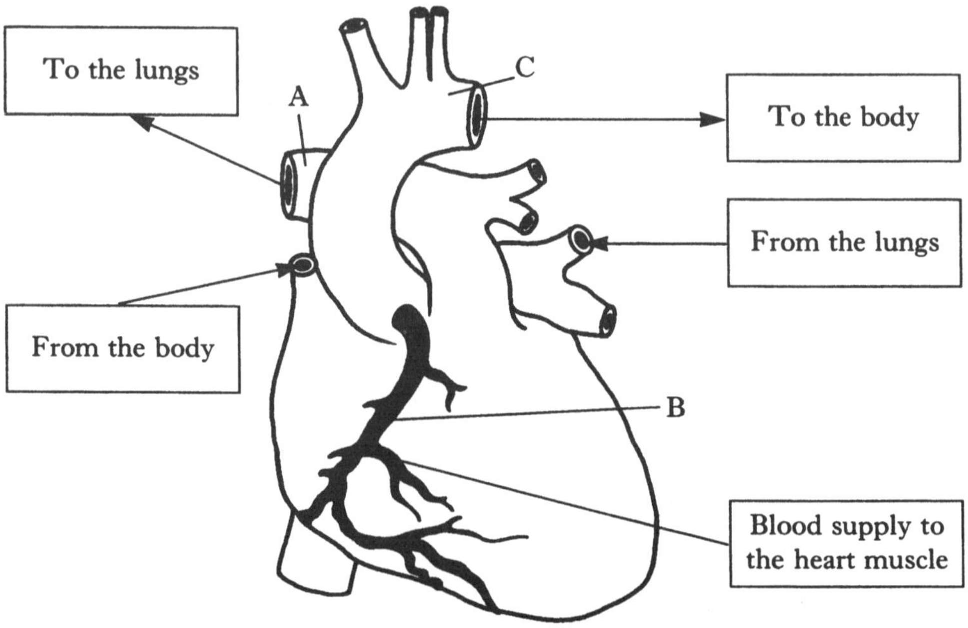


Complete the table below to show whether the blood in vessels A, B and C is oxygenated (high oxygen concentration) or deoxygenated (low oxygen concentration) by placing a tick (✓) in the correct column.

| *Vessel* | *Oxygenated blood* | *Deoxygenated blood* |
|---|---|---|
| A | | |
| B | | |
| C | | |

**(2)**

Candidates must not write in this margin

*Marks*

**12.** (*a*) The diagram below shows the nerve cells (neurones) involved in a reflex arc through the spinal cord.

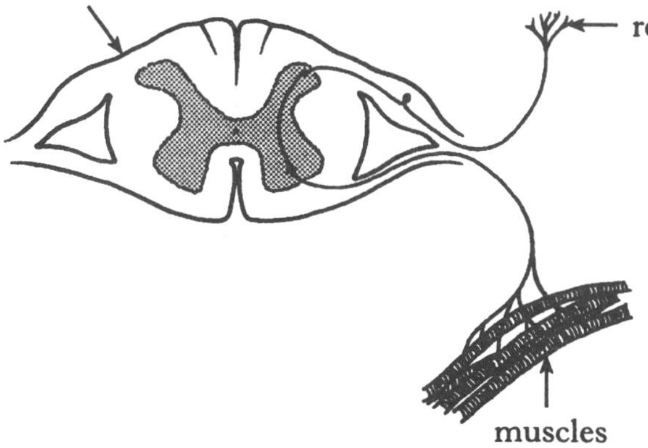


The incomplete list below contains descriptions of some of the stages in a reflex action.

Stage 1 Detection of stimulus by receptor

Stage 2 ____________________

Stage 3 Impulse sent along relay fibre

Stage 4 ____________________

Stage 5 Response made by effector organ

Complete the list by describing stages 2 and 4.

Stage 2 ______________________________

Stage 4 ______________________________ **(2)**

(*b*) Complete the table below by inserting R against those responses which are reflex actions.

| *Responses* | |
|---|---|
| Pupil of the eye gets smaller in bright light | |
| Eating when hungry | |
| Running cold water over a burnt hand | |
| Swallowing when food touches the back of the throat | |

**(2)**

Candidates must not write in this margin

*Marks*

**13.** A single-celled organism is found living in the water of an estuary where the salt concentration of the water is constantly changing.

The changes in the salt concentration are observed to cause volume changes in the organism.

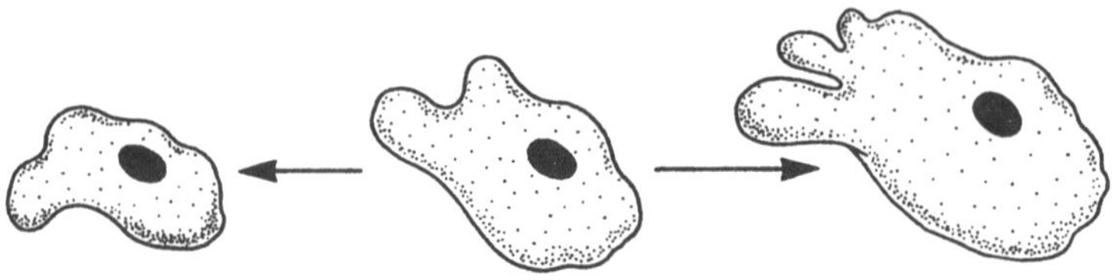

(*a*) The volume changes are due to the movement of water in and out of the organism by osmosis.

Describe what is meant by the term *osmosis*.

______________________________

______________________________

______________________________ **(1)**

(*b*) When the tide comes in, the organism undergoes the volume change shown below.

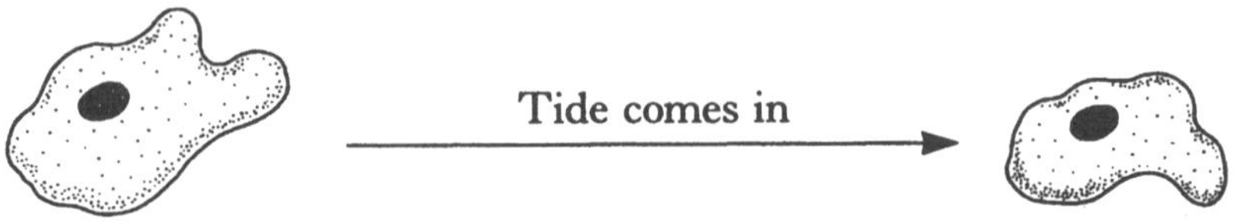


Underline **one** word in the set of brackets to make the sentence correct.

The organism is now surrounded by {a hypotonic / an isotonic / a hypertonic} solution. **(1)**

(*c*) This organism depends on the process of diffusion.

Explain the importance of diffusion to organisms.

______________________________

______________________________

______________________________ **(1)**

Candidates must not write in this margin

## SECTION C

Marks

**Answer BOTH questions 1 and 2 on the blank pages provided.**

**You may use labelled diagrams where appropriate.**

1. Answer **either** A **or** B.

A. The diagrams below show a bacterial cell and part of a human chromosome.

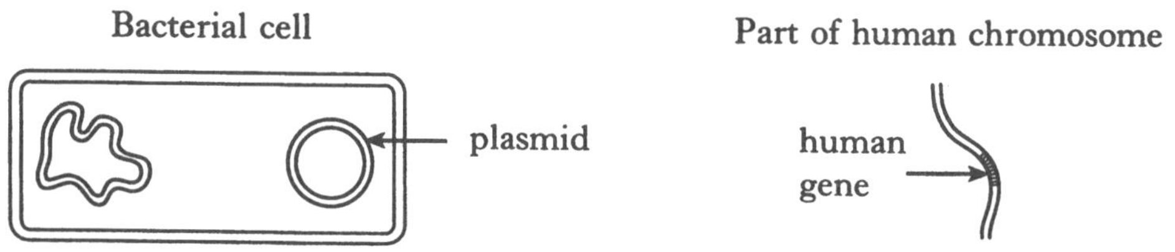


Genetic engineering can be used to produce bacterial cells capable of making a human protein.

Describe the steps carried out to produce bacterial cells containing a human gene. **(5)**

**OR**

B. The diagram below shows a kidney nephron.

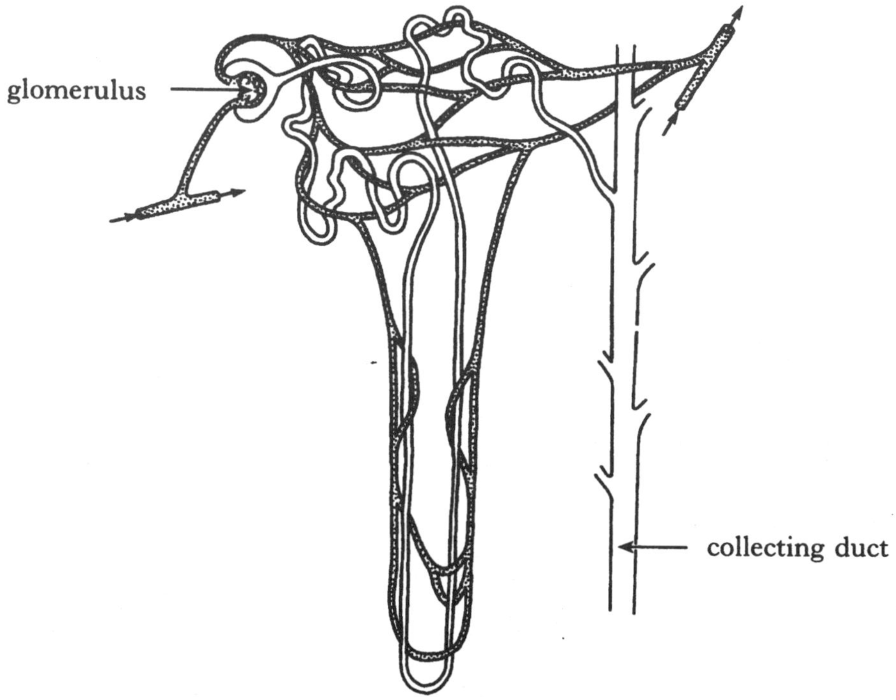


Give an account of what happens to both glucose and urea molecules in the blood entering the glomerulus of a kidney nephron. **(5)**

Candidates must not write in this margin

**2.** Answer **either** A **or** B.

*Marks*

A. Give an account of the breakdown of glucose and the production of ATP during aerobic respiration. **(5)**

**OR**

B. Describe how pollution can affect the variety of species in an ecosystem. **(5)**

[*END OF QUESTION PAPER*]

SPACE FOR ANSWERS

ADDITIONAL GRAPH PAPER FOR QUESTION 5(*a*)(i)

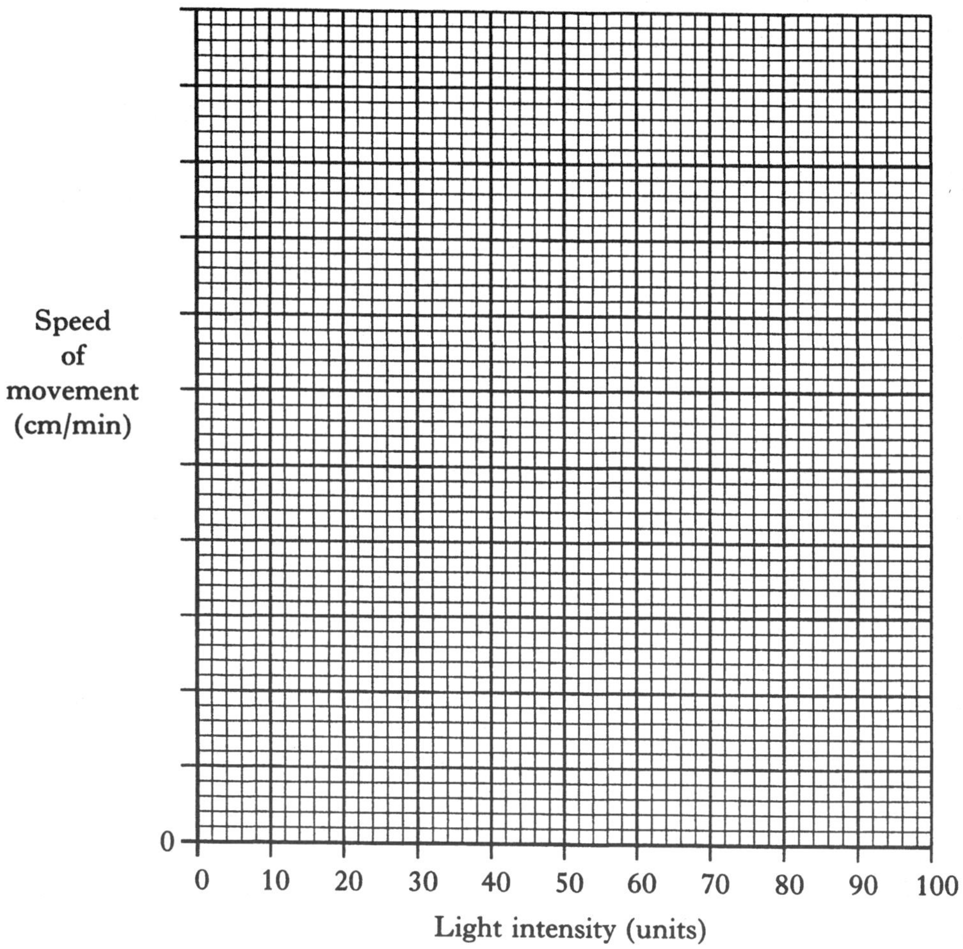

# INTERMEDIATE 2 2000

FOR OFFICIAL USE

| | | | | | |
|---|---|---|---|---|---|
| | | | | | |

# X007/201

NATIONAL QUALIFICATIONS 2000

MONDAY, 29 MAY
9.00 AM – 11.00 AM

# BIOLOGY
## INTERMEDIATE 2

**Fill in these boxes and read what is printed below.**

Full name of centre

Town

Forename(s)

Surname

Date of birth
Day Month Year

Scottish candidate number

Number of seat

**SECTION A (25 marks)**
Instructions for completion of Section A are given on page two.

**SECTIONS B AND C (75 marks)**

1 (a) All questions should be attempted.
  (b) It should be noted that in **Section C** questions 1 and 2 each contain a choice.

2 The questions may be answered in any order but all answers are to be written in the spaces provided in this answer book, and must be written clearly and legibly in ink.

3 Additional space for answers and rough work will be found at the end of the book. If further space is required, supplementary sheets may be obtained from the invigilator and should be inserted inside the **front** cover of this book.

4 The numbers of questions must be clearly inserted with any answers written in the additional space.

5 Rough work, if any should be necessary, should be written in this book and then scored through when the fair copy has been written.

6 Before leaving the examination room you must give this book to the invigilator. If you do not, you may lose all the marks for this paper.

SCOTTISH QUALIFICATIONS AUTHORITY

**Read carefully**

1 Check that the answer sheet provided is for Biology Intermediate 2 (Section A).

2 Fill in the details required on the answer sheet.

3 In this section a question is answered by indicating the choice A, B, C or D by a stroke made in **ink** in the appropriate place in the answer sheet—see the sample question below.

4 For each question there is only **one** correct answer.

5 Rough working, if required, should be done only on this question paper, or on the rough working sheet provided—**not** on the answer sheet.

6 At the end of the examination the answer sheet for Section A **must** be placed inside the front cover of this answer book.

**Sample Question**

Which of the following are the raw materials for photosynthesis?

A Carbon dioxide and glucose

B Carbon dioxide and water

C Oxygen and water

D Oxygen and glucose

**The correct answer is B**—carbon dioxide and water. A **heavy** vertical line should be drawn joining the two dots in the appropriate box in the column headed **B** as shown **in the example on the answer sheet**.

If, after you have recorded your answer, you decide that you have made an error and wish to make a change, you should cancel the original answer and put a vertical stroke in the box you now consider to be correct. Thus, if you want to change an answer **D** to an answer **B**, your answer sheet would look like this:

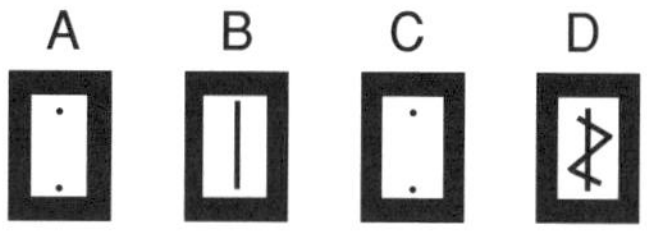


If you want to change back to an answer which has already been scored out, you should **enter a tick (✓)** to the RIGHT of the box of your choice, thus:

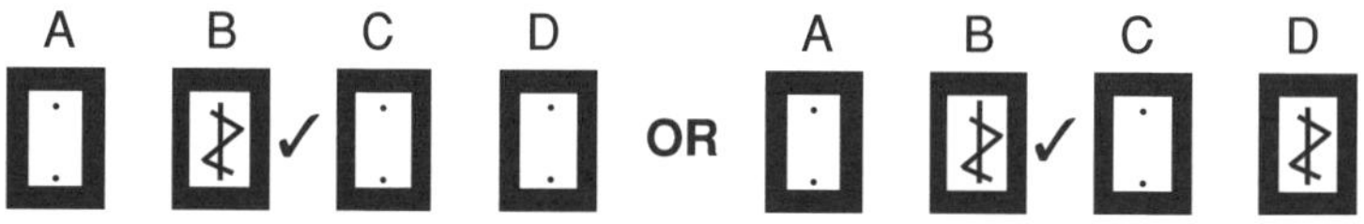

## SECTION A

**All questions in this Section should be attempted.**

**1.** Which of the following lists all the elements that are present in every protein molecule?

A Carbon, hydrogen, oxygen, nitrogen

B Carbon, oxygen, nitrogen

C Carbon, hydrogen, oxygen, sulphur

D Carbon, hydrogen, oxygen

**2.** The table below shows some of the features of blood vessels.

Which line describes features of arteries?

| | *Direction of blood flow* | *Detection of pulse* | *Presence of valves* |
|---|---|---|---|
| A | Towards the heart | Yes | No |
| B | Away from the heart | No | Yes |
| C | Towards the heart | No | Yes |
| D | Away from the heart | Yes | No |

**Questions 3 and 4** refer to the diagram below which shows the human brain.

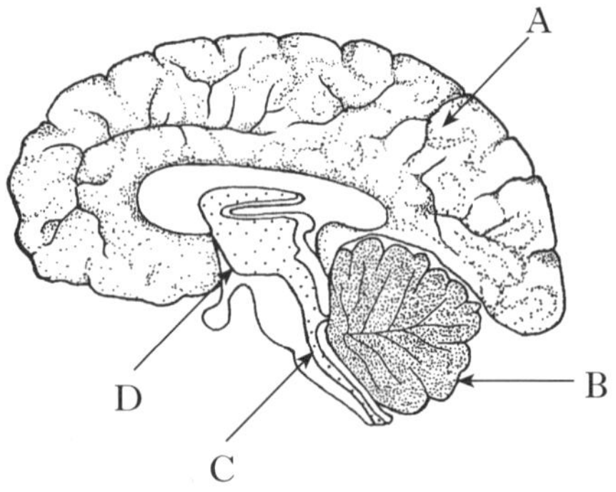


**3.** Which labelled arrow is pointing to the cerebellum?

**4.** Which labelled part is the site of temperature regulation?

**5.** Which of the diagrams below describes negative feedback control by anti-diuretic hormone (ADH)?

A

More ADH released → Decrease in water concentration of the blood → Less ADH released → Increase in water concentration of the blood → More ADH released

B

Less ADH released → Decrease in water concentration of the blood → More ADH released → Increase in water concentration of the blood → Less ADH released

C

More ADH released → Increase in water concentration of the blood → Less ADH released → Increase in water concentration of the blood → More ADH released

D

Less ADH released → Decrease in water concentration of the blood → More ADH released → Decrease in water concentration of the blood → Less ADH released

**6.** The graph below shows the effect of temperature on the rate of photosynthesis in a plant.

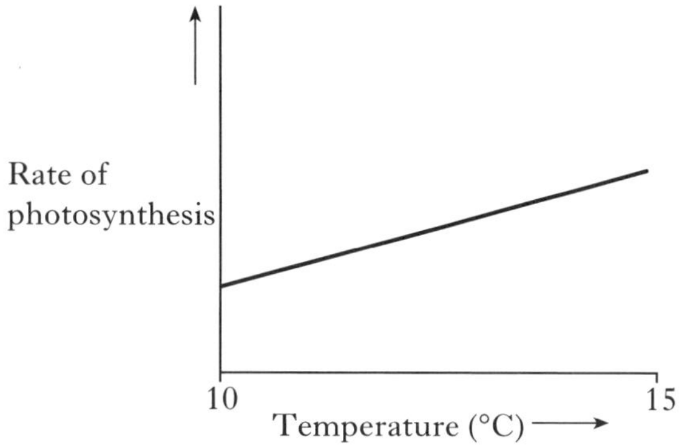


A correct conclusion would be that

A as the temperature increases, the rate of photosynthesis increases

B as the temperature increases, the rate of photosynthesis decreases

C as the temperature increases, the rate of photosynthesis remains constant

D as the temperature decreases, the rate of photosynthesis increases.

**7.** The graph below shows the effect of increasing light intensity on the rate of photosynthesis.

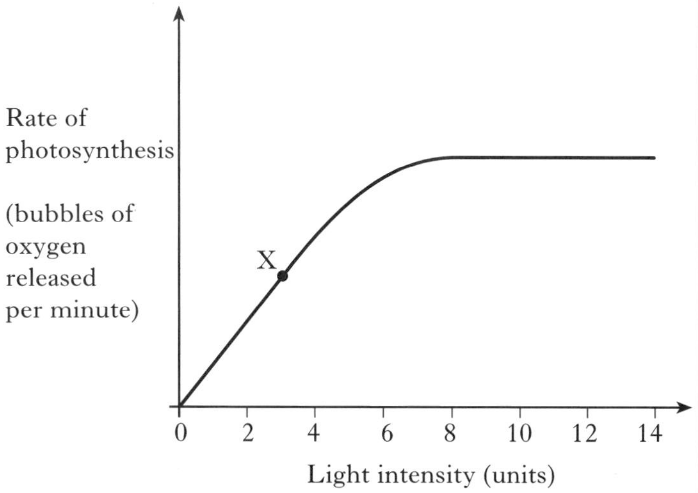


Which factor is limiting the rate of photosynthesis at point X on the graph?

A Carbon dioxide concentration

B Temperature

C Light intensity

D Oxygen concentration

**8.** The diagram below shows a food web from the seashore.

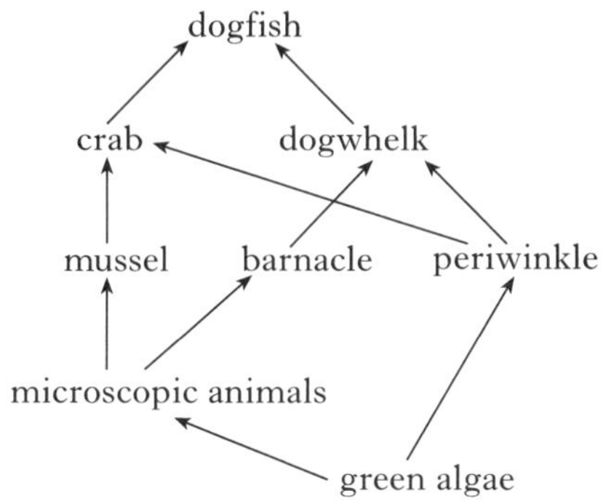


The mussel can be described as a

A producer

B primary consumer

C secondary consumer

D decomposer.

**9.** Plants convert 1% of the light energy they receive into new plant material.

In the food chain below, primroses receive 100 000 units of light energy.

Primrose ⟶ vole ⟶ weasel ⟶ owl

How much of this energy is converted into new plant material?

A 10 000 units

B 1000 units

C 100 units

D 10 units

**10.** Which of the following describes a population in an ecosystem?

A The total number of one species present

B All the living organisms and the non-living parts of the ecosystem

C All the living organisms

D All the plants

**11.** Which term refers to the process by which organisms that are better adapted to their environment survive and breed?

A Meiosis

B Natural selection

C Selective breeding

D Genetic engineering

**12.** When the body is starved of food it has to rely on its food reserves to provide energy.

The first food reserves to be used are carbohydrates, then fats; after several weeks of starvation, proteins are used.

Which of the graphs below shows what would happen to the food reserves if an individual was starved for several weeks?

**Key**
carbohydrate ————
fat — — — —
protein ○ ○ ○ ○ ○ ○

A

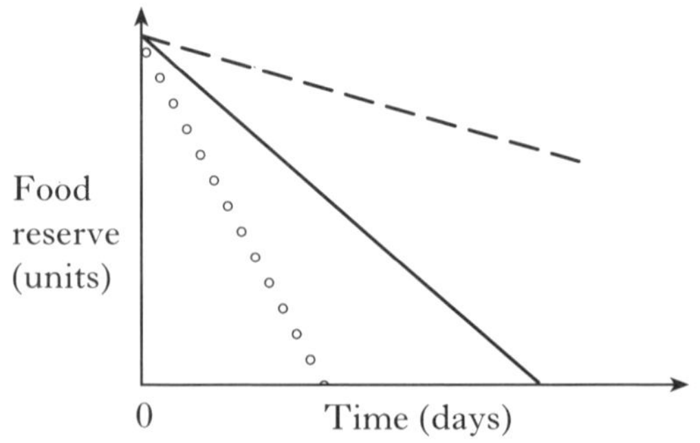


B

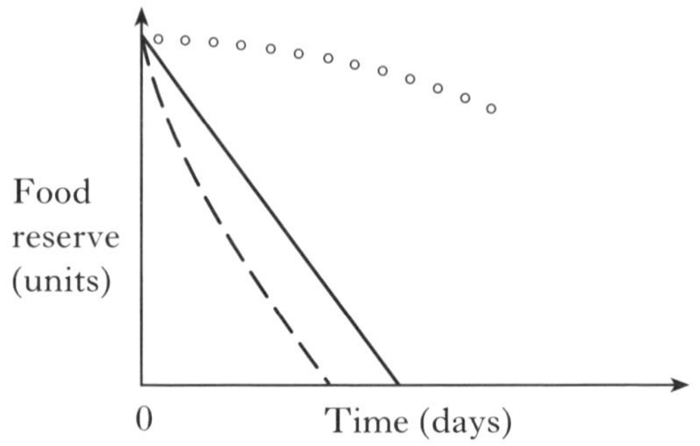


C

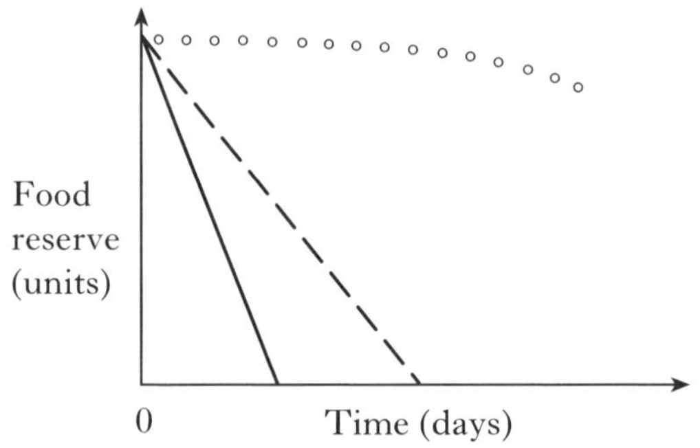


D

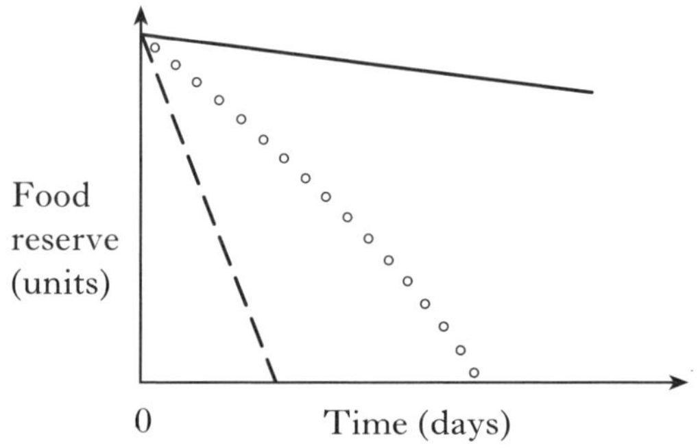


**13.** A garden pond has snails, goldfish, water lilies and some pondweed living in it.

Students monitored the oxygen concentration of the water and found that it was too low.

Which of the following changes should they make to increase the oxygen concentration of the water?

A Remove some snails and add more goldfish

B Remove some snails and add more pondweed

C Remove some pondweed and add more snails

D Remove some water lilies and add more goldfish

**14.** Which of the following shows the use of energy released from the breakdown of glucose?

A ATP + Pi → ADP

B ADP + Pi → ATP

C ATP → ADP + Pi

D ADP → ATP + Pi

**15.** The movement of water through a selectively permeable membrane from an area of high water concentration to an area of low water concentration is called

A absorption

B osmosis

C plasmolysis

D filtration.

**[Turn over**

**Questions 16 and 17** refer to the information below.

In mice, the dominant form (B) of one gene determines black coat colour; brown coat colour results from the recessive form (b) of the gene.

A cross between two mice is shown below.

P BB × bb

$F_1$ Bb

**16.** Which of the following shows all the possible genotypes of the $F_2$ generation?

A BB and Bb

B bb and Bb

C BB and bb

D BB, Bb and bb

**17.** What proportion of the $F_2$ generation would be expected to have black coats?

A $\frac{1}{4}$

B $\frac{1}{2}$

C $\frac{2}{3}$

D $\frac{3}{4}$

**18.** In humans, which of the following gametes would determine a male offspring at fertilisation?

A An egg cell with an X chromosome

B An egg cell with a Y chromosome

C A sperm cell with an X chromosome

D A sperm cell with a Y chromosome

**19.** Which line in the table below names gametes and their sites of production in a flowering plant?

| | *Male gamete* | *Site of production* | *Female gamete* | *Site of production* |
|---|---|---|---|---|
| A | Sperm | testes | egg | ovule |
| B | Pollen nucleus | anther | egg cell | ovary |
| C | Sperm | anther | egg | ovary |
| D | Pollen nucleus | testes | egg cell | ovule |

**20.** Which term refers to a description of a characteristic of an organism?

A Genotype

B Phenotype

C Allele

D Natural selection

**21.** Which term refers to forms of a gene controlling the same characteristic?

A Genotypes

B Phenotypes

C Alleles

D Dominant

**Questions 22, 23 and 24** refer to the information below.

An investigation into the effect of pH on the digestion of milk by an enzyme was carried out.

Five identical dishes were set up with wells cut out of the agar.

To each well was added 5 $cm^3$ of the enzyme kept at a different pH as shown in the diagram below.

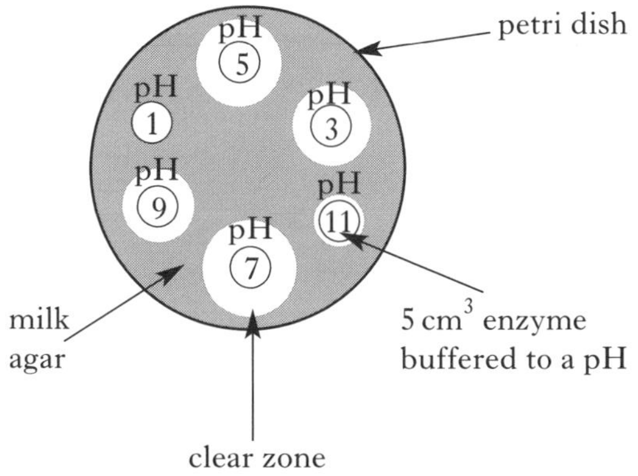


The dishes were kept at 35 °C.

The diameter of the area cleared by the action of the enzyme was measured.

| | *Diameter of clear zone* (mm) | | | | |
|---|---|---|---|---|---|
| *pH* | *Dish 1* | *Dish 2* | *Dish 3* | *Dish 4* | *Dish 5* |
| 1 | 0 | 0 | 0 | 0 | 0 |
| 3 | 2 | 1 | 1 | 2 | 1 |
| 5 | 3 | 4 | 2 | 3 | 3 |
| 7 | 6 | 5 | 5 | 5 | 4 |
| 9 | 2 | 2 | 3 | 1 | 2 |
| 11 | 1 | 0 | 0 | 1 | 0 |

**22.** The average diameter cleared at pH 5 was

A 3 mm

B 4 mm

C 5 mm

D 6 mm.

**23.** The variable altered in this investigation was

A temperature

B diameter of the well

C pH

D milk concentration.

**24.** The pH at which the enzyme was most active was

A 3

B 5

C 7

D 9.

**25.** Which of the graphs below shows the effect of increasing temperature on enzyme activity?

A

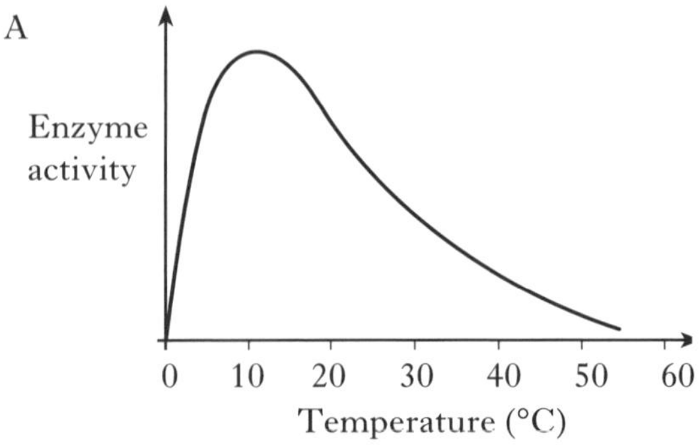


B

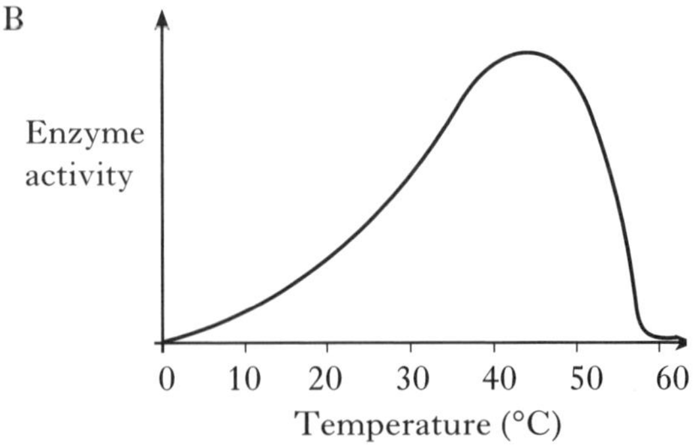


C

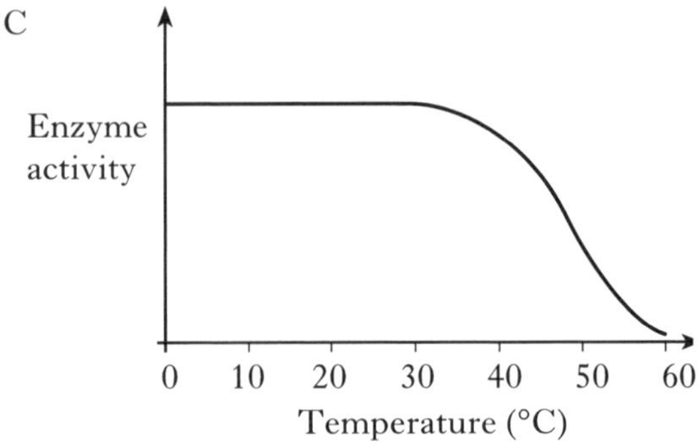


D

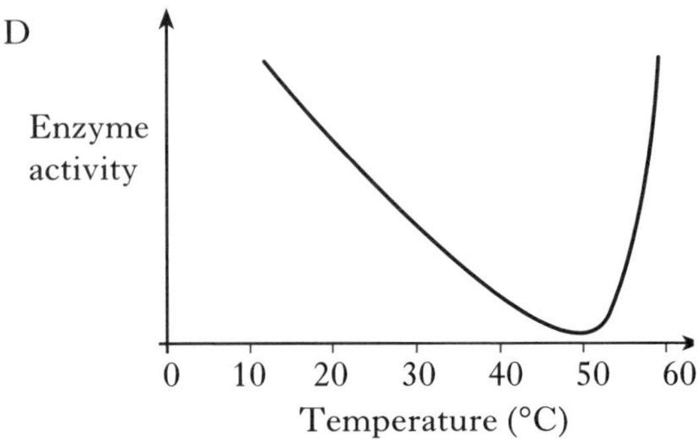


**Candidates are reminded that the answer sheet for Section A MUST be placed <u>inside</u> the front cover of this answer book.**

DO NOT WRITE IN THIS MARGIN

## SECTION B

**All questions in this section should be attempted.**

*Marks*

1. The diagram below shows the pyramid of numbers for a food chain of a coastal bay.

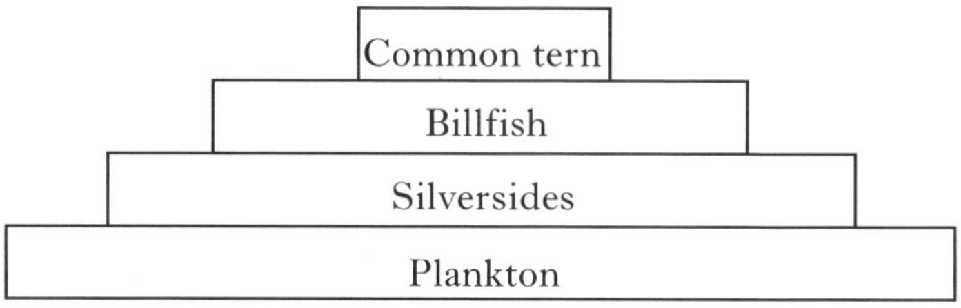


(*a*) (i) Present the information in the diagram as a food chain.

______________________________ 1

(ii) Use the diagram above to explain what is meant by the term *pyramid of numbers*.

______________________________

______________________________

______________________________ 2

(*b*) What other feature of a food chain can be represented as a pyramid?

______________________________ 1

DO NOT WRITE IN THIS MARGIN

*Marks*

**2.** The diagram below shows some steps in respiration in muscle cells.

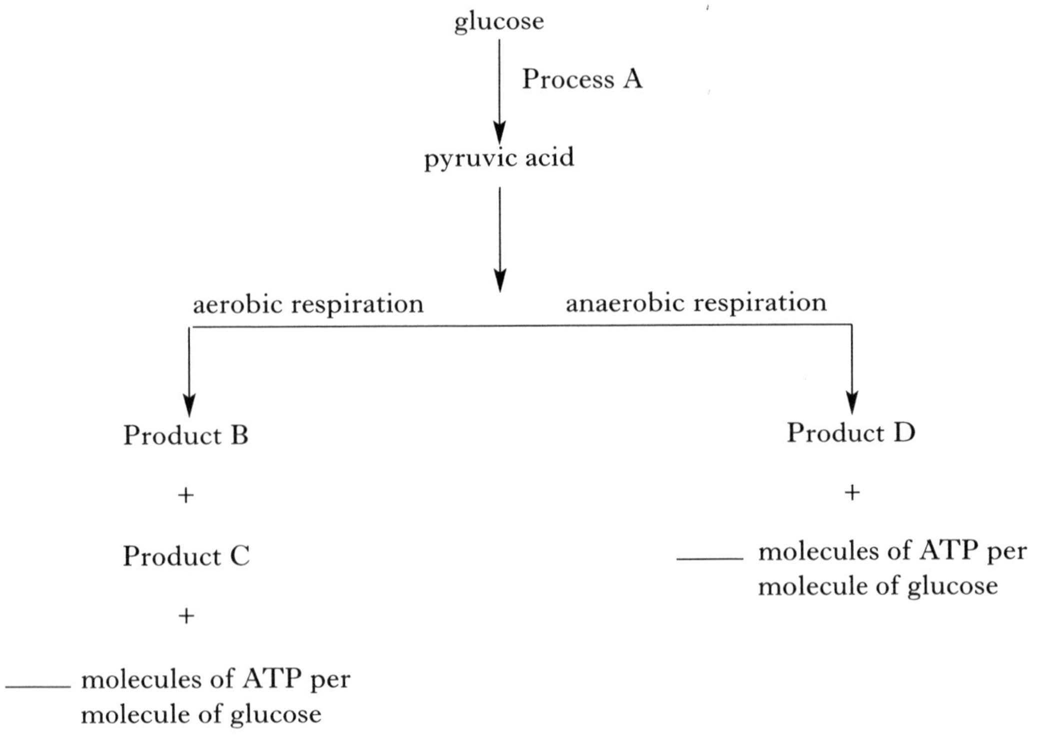


(*a*) Name Process A.

____________________________________ **1**

(*b*) Name the products B, C and D.

B ____________________________________

C ____________________________________

D ____________________________________ **2**

(*c*) State the number of molecules of ATP produced from each molecule of glucose by

(i) aerobic respiration ____________________

(ii) anaerobic respiration. ____________________ **1**

(*d*) Why might a muscle cell switch from aerobic to anaerobic respiration?

____________________________________________________________________ **1**

DO NOT WRITE IN THIS MARGIN

*Marks*

**3.** The diagram below represents a kidney nephron.

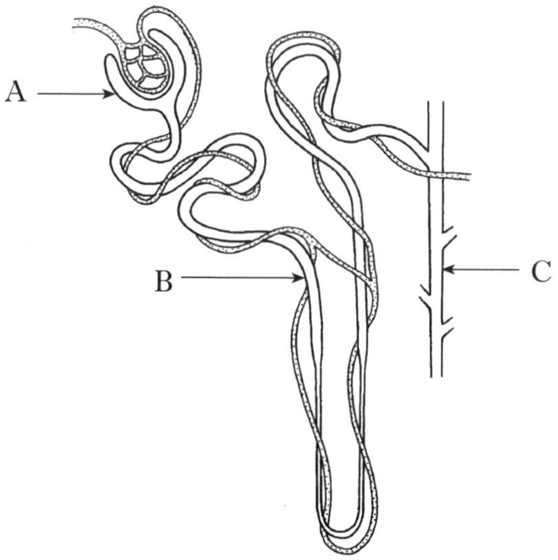


(*a*) (i) Name the processes which take place in the areas labelled A and B.

A ______________________________

B ______________________________ **2**

(ii) Name the structure labelled C.

______________________________ **1**

(*b*) Excess protein in the body is broken down in the liver.
Name the waste product formed from the breakdown of protein.

______________________________ **1**

(*c*) Describe the effect on the kidney tubules of an increasing level of anti-diuretic hormone (ADH).

______________________________ **1**

DO NOT WRITE IN THIS MARGIN

Marks

**3. (continued)**

(*d*) Bony fish can live in freshwater or marine habitats.

The list below contains methods used by bony fish to overcome osmotic problems.

*Methods used by bony fish to overcome osmotic problems*
Excreting excess salt
Excreting copious urine
Producing very dilute urine
Drinking water

Use all the information above to complete the table.

| *Habitat* | *Osmotic problem* | *Methods used by bony fish to overcome the osmotic problem* |
|---|---|---|
| | Water gain | |
| | Water loss | |

3

**[Turn over**

DO NOT WRITE IN THIS MARGIN

*Marks*

4. (*a*) The table below shows some substances that are transported in the blood.

Tick (✓) the correct box(es) to show the part(s) of the blood in which each substance is transported.

| *Substance* | *Part of blood* | |
|---|---|---|
| | *Plasma* | *Red blood cells* |
| Oxygen | | |
| Carbon dioxide | | |
| Amino acids | | |
| Glucose | | |

2

(*b*) The graph below shows the percentage saturation of a solution of haemoglobin plotted against the concentration of oxygen dissolved in the surrounding fluid.

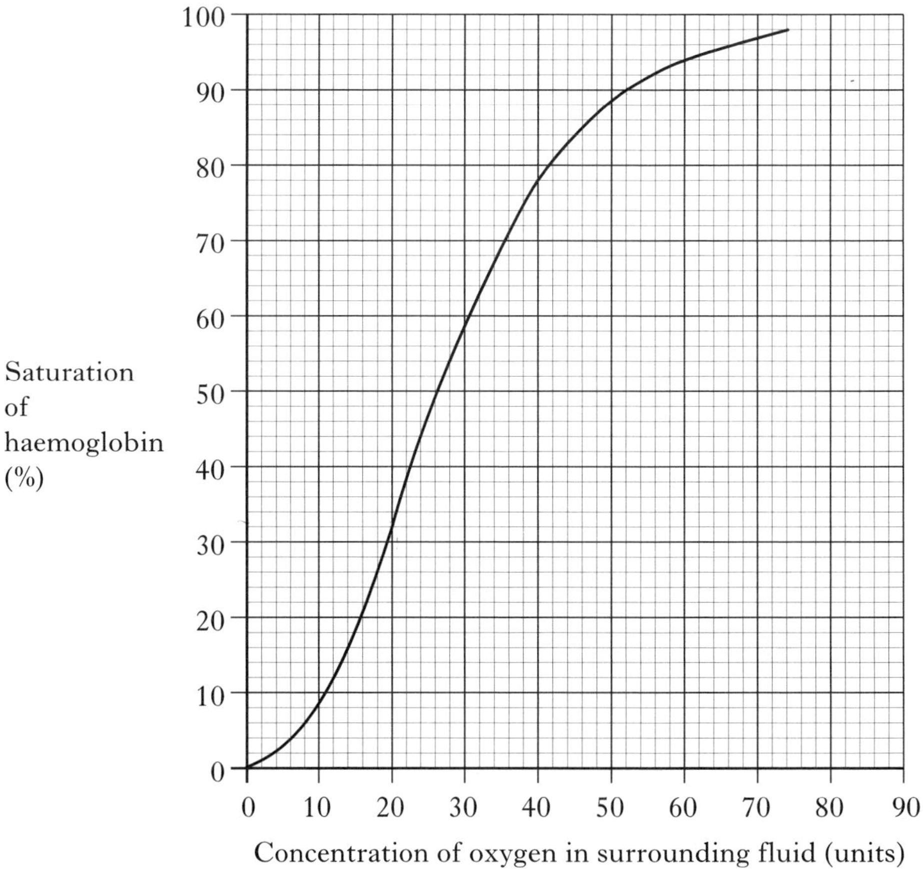

DO NOT WRITE IN THIS MARGIN

*Marks*

**4. (*b*) (continued)**

(i) What is the percentage saturation of haemoglobin when the oxygen concentration is 20 units in the surrounding fluid?

____________________% **1**

(ii) What is the concentration of oxygen in the surrounding fluid when the percentage saturation of haemoglobin is 90%?

____________________units **1**

(iii) Describe the relationship between the oxygen concentration of the surrounding fluid and the percentage saturation of haemoglobin.

________________________________________

________________________________________ **1**

(*c*) Oxygen is used up in respiration in the tissues of the body.

Describe the effect of low oxygen concentration in the tissues on oxyhaemoglobin in the blood in the capillaries.

________________________________________

________________________________________ **1**

**[Turn over**

*Marks*

**5.** Yeast cells contain the enzyme catalase which breaks down hydrogen peroxide into oxygen and water.

Hydrogen peroxide $\xrightarrow{\text{catalase}}$ oxygen + water

The following diagram and description outlines how an investigation was set up and carried out.

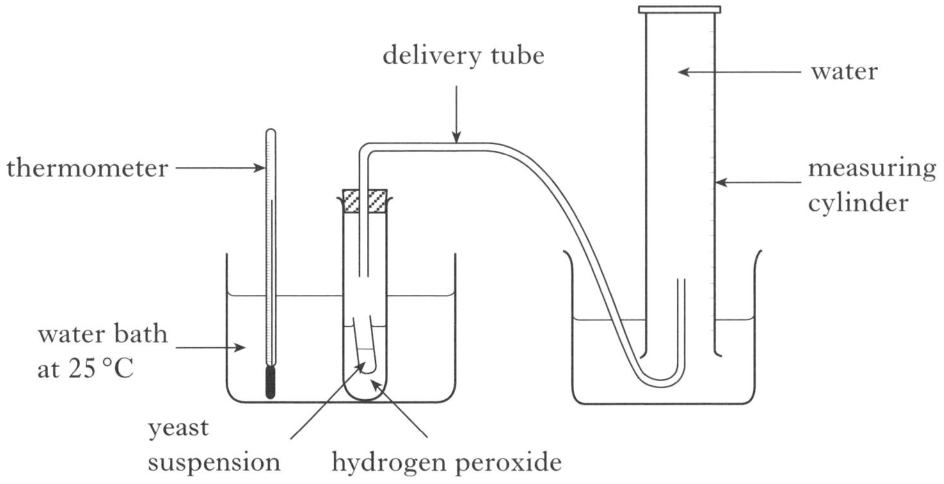


After ten minutes in the water bath at 25 °C, the yeast suspension was mixed with the hydrogen peroxide by shaking the test-tube.

The volume of oxygen released from the hydrogen peroxide in one minute was measured.

The procedure was then repeated at 25 °C.

The same apparatus was then used to investigate the effect of a range of temperatures.

(*a*) In this investigation temperature is the only variable which should be changed.

State **two** variables which should be constant.

1 ________________________________

2 ________________________________ **2**

(*b*) (i) Explain why the procedure was repeated at each temperature and an average calculated.

________________________________________________ **1**

(ii) Explain why the yeast and hydrogen peroxide were not mixed **before** they were placed in the water bath.

________________________________________________ **1**

*Marks*

**5. (continued)**

(*c*) The results are shown in the table below.

| *Temperature* (°C) | *Volume of oxygen collected* ($cm^3$/minute) | | |
|---|---|---|---|
| | *First run* | *Second run* | *Average* |
| 25 | 15 | 15 | 15 |
| 30 | 20 | 22 | 21 |
| 35 | 36 | 40 | 38 |
| 40 | 46 | 46 | 46 |
| 45 | 10 | 8 | 9 |
| 50 | 0 | 0 | 0 |
| 60 | 0 | 0 | 0 |

Present the results in an appropriate format on the grid below.

(Additional graph paper, if required, will be found on page 28.)

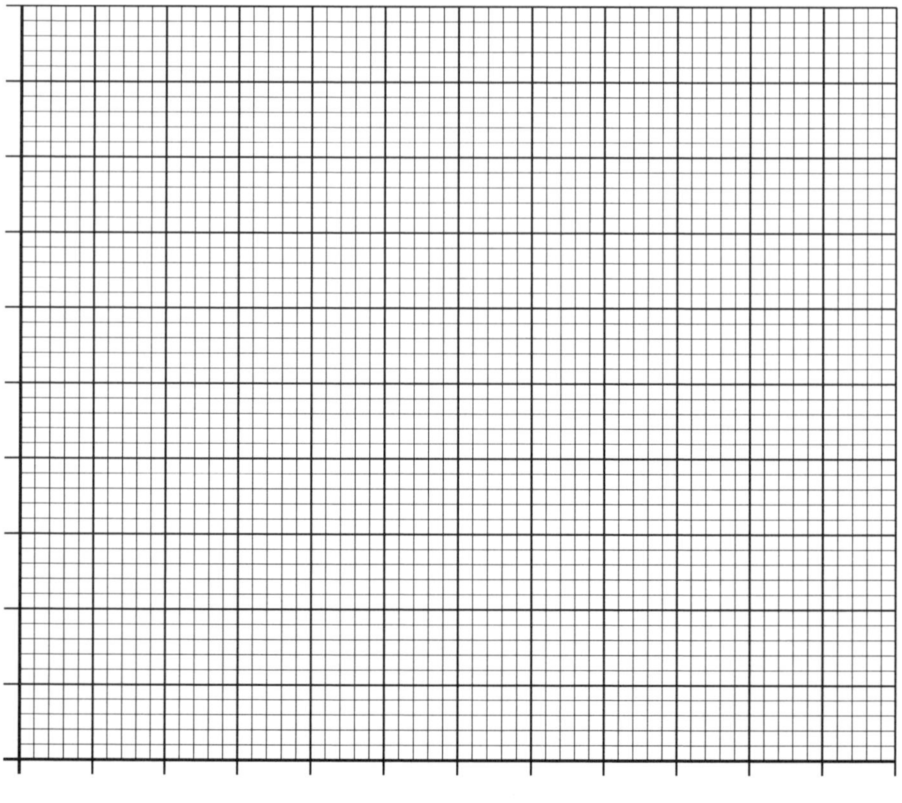

**3**

DO NOT WRITE IN THIS MARGIN

*Marks*

**6.** (*a*) Three similar cylinders were cut from the same potato, dried and weighed. Each cylinder was placed in a different solution as shown in the diagrams below.

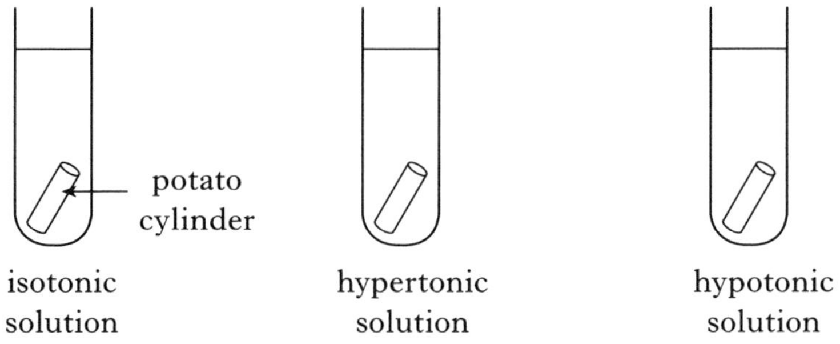


After one hour, the cylinders were removed from the solutions, dried and reweighed.

(i) Use the information in the diagrams to complete the table below.

| *Solution* | *Initial weight* (g) | *Final weight* (g) |
|---|---|---|
| | 10 | 8 |
| | 10 | 10 |
| | 10 | 12 |

**1**

(ii) Which process has caused these changes in weight?

________________________________ **1**

(iii) The diagram below shows a cell from one of the potato cylinders.

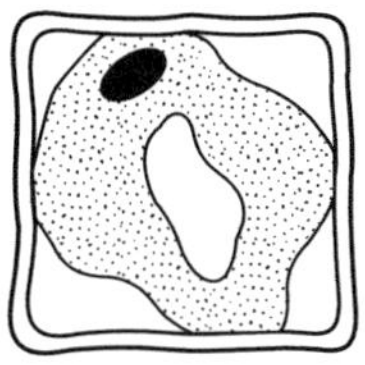

What term would be used to describe the condition of this cell?

________________________________ **1**

DO NOT WRITE IN THIS MARGIN

*Marks*

**6. (continued)**

(*b*) (i) Some structures that are found in cells are listed below.

Tick (✓) boxes to show those structures which are found in animal cells.

| | |
|---|---|
| Chloroplasts | ☐ |
| Cytoplasm | ☐ |
| Large central vacuole | ☐ |
| Cell wall | ☐ |
| Nucleus | ☐ |
| Cell membrane | ☐ |

**1**

(ii) Explain why diffusion is important to a unicellular animal such as *Amoeba*.

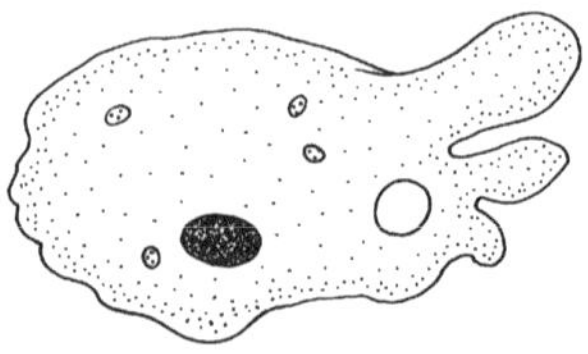

______________________________________________

______________________________________________ **1**

**[Turn over**

Marks

**7.** Potatoes store carbohydrate in the form of starch.

An enzyme found in potato cells converts glucose-1-phosphate into starch.

$$\text{glucose-1-phosphate} \xrightarrow{\text{Enzyme}} \text{starch}$$

The following description outlines how an investigation into the time taken for the synthesis of starch to occur was carried out.

1 A starch-free potato extract was prepared.
This potato extract contained the enzyme.

2 Two rows of a spotting tile were set up as shown in the diagram.

A

B

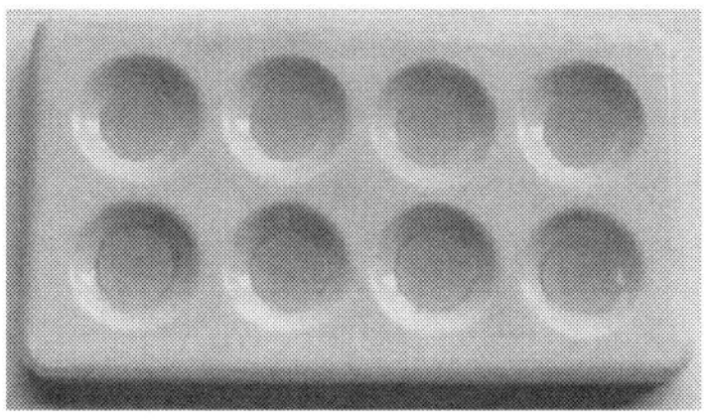

glucose-1-phosphate + potato extract

glucose-1-phosphate + water

3 A stop clock was started.

4 Iodine was added to each column at 5 minute intervals.
Iodine turns black when starch is present.

The results are shown below.

A

B

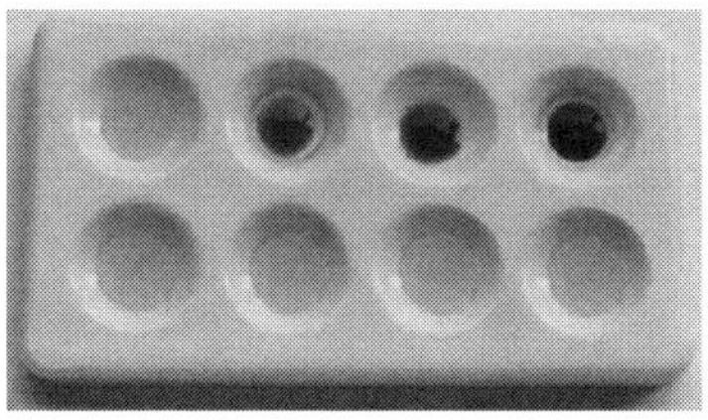

5 10 15 20

Time (minutes)

DO NOT WRITE IN THIS MARGIN

*Marks*

**7. (continued)**

(*a*) Name the enzyme present in the potato extract.

__________________________ **1**

(*b*) Explain why all the starch was removed from the potato extract before it was used in the investigation.

________________________________________________

________________________________________________ **1**

(*c*) What evidence is there to show that the enzyme is necessary for the synthesis of starch?

________________________________________________ **1**

(*d*) What conclusion can be drawn from the results in row A?

________________________________________________ **1**

**[Turn over**

DO NOT WRITE IN THIS MARGIN

Marks

**8.** The diagram below shows a single villus from the small intestine.

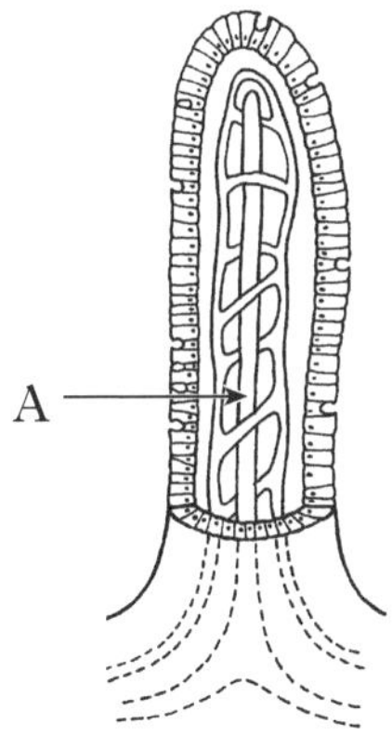


(*a*) Name the part labelled A.

________________________________ **1**

(*b*) Absorption of glucose takes place in the small intestine.

(i) Name the part of the villus into which glucose passes.

________________________________ **1**

(ii) Name the organ to which the glucose is transported after leaving the small intestine.

________________________________ **1**

(iii) Describe **one** possible use of glucose in the body.

____________________________________________________ **1**

(*c*) The stomach is a major organ of the alimentary canal.

(i) Name **two** types of secretory cell found in the stomach.

1 ________________________________

2 ________________________________ **2**

(ii) Describe the function of the muscles in the stomach wall.

____________________________________________________ **1**

DO NOT WRITE IN THIS MARGIN

*Marks*

**9.** The diagram below shows the occurrence of tongue rolling in a family.

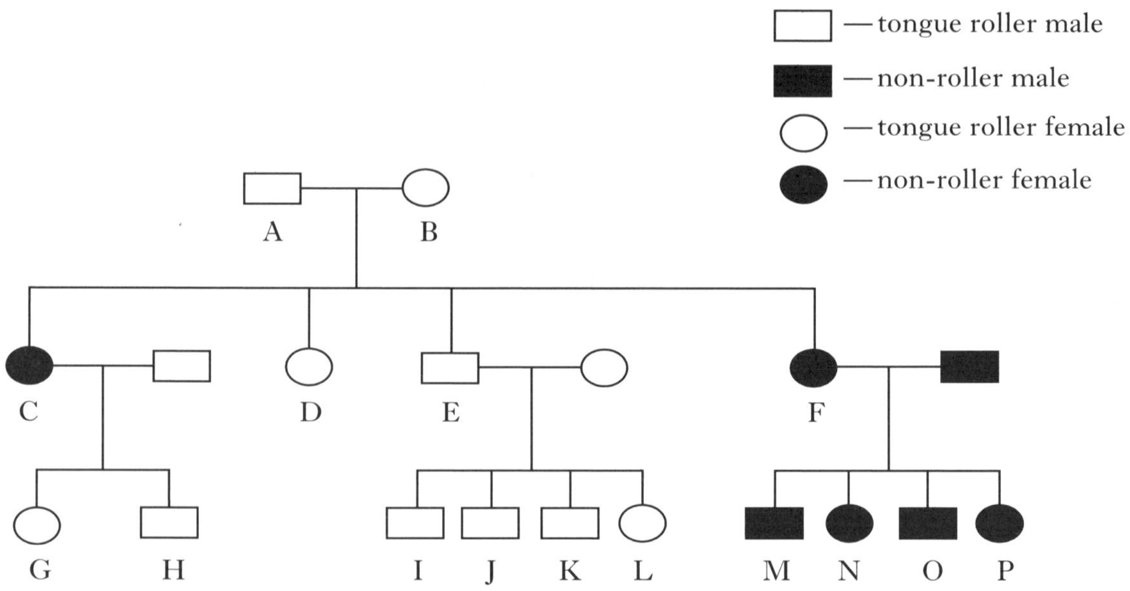


(*a*) State the dominant form of the gene.

______________________________________ **1**

(*b*) Identify the individuals in the $F_1$ generation.

______________________________________ **1**

(*c*) (i) Use the information in the diagram to complete the table below.

| *Individual* | *Genotype* |
|---|---|
| A | |
| B | Tt |
| C | |
| G | |
| L | TT |

**3**

(ii) Name an individual from the table who is heterozygous for the gene.

______________________________________ **1**

**[Turn over**

DO NOT WRITE IN THIS MARGIN

*Marks*

**10.** The apparatus shown below was set up to investigate the response of a small freshwater organism called *Daphnia* to an environmental factor.

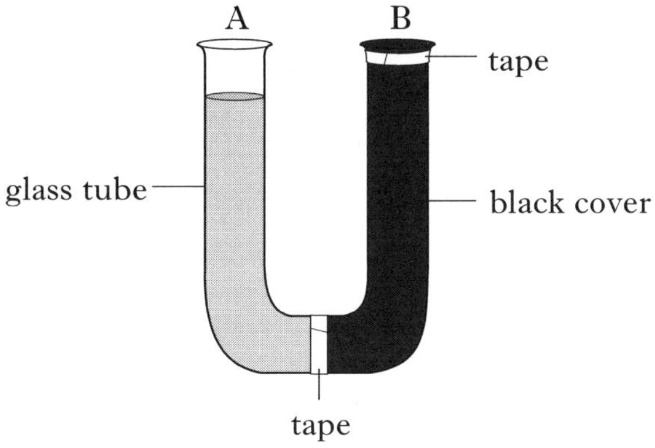


Fifteen *Daphnia* were placed in each side of the glass tube and allowed to swim around for 10 minutes.

A black cover was then placed over side B.

The number of *Daphnia* in each side was then counted at 5 minute intervals for 30 minutes.

The results are shown below.

| *Time* (minutes) | *Number of Daphnia in side A* | *Number of Daphnia in side B* |
|---|---|---|
| 0 | 15 | 15 |
| 5 | 25 | 5 |
| 10 | 27 | 3 |
| 15 | 24 | 6 |
| 20 | 28 | 2 |
| 25 | 28 | 2 |
| 30 | 29 | 1 |

(*a*) Name the environmental factor causing the response.

__________________________________ **1**

(*b*) Express, as a simple ratio, the number of *Daphnia* on side A to the number on side B after 10 minutes.
*Space for calculation*

___________ : ___________ **1**

DO NOT WRITE IN THIS MARGIN

*Marks*

**10. (continued)**

(*c*) What conclusion can be drawn from these results?

______________________________________ **1**

(*d*) *Daphnia* feed on green algae at the surface of the water.

Explain the significance of the behaviour observed in this investigation to *Daphnia*.

______________________________________

______________________________________ **1**

**[Turn over**

*Marks*

**11.** (*a*) Some students were asked to design an investigation to compare the rate of production of oxygen gas by two different species of water plant.

The diagrams below show the proposed procedure.

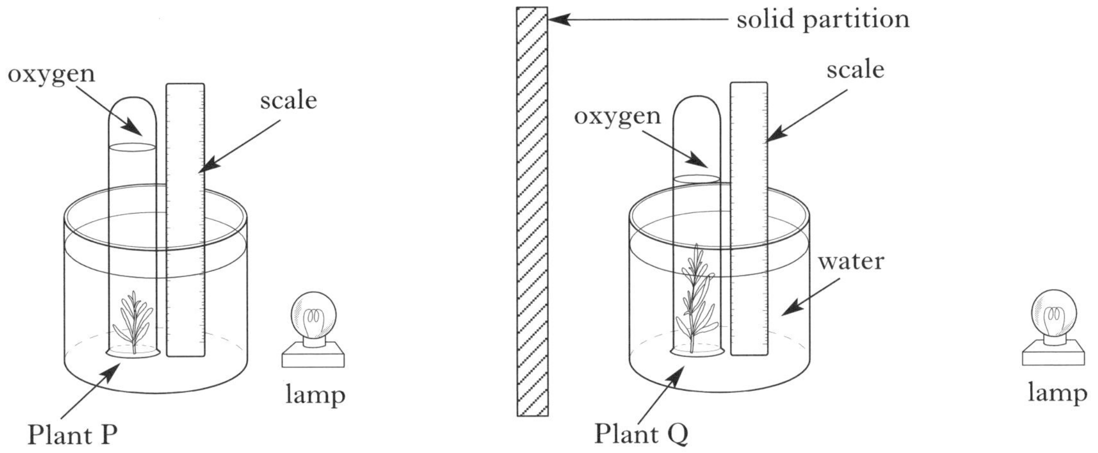


Identify **two** changes to the procedure that should be made to ensure that a valid conclusion can be made.

1 ________________________________________

2 ________________________________________ **2**

(*b*) When changes were made to ensure validity, the following results were obtained.

| *Plant* | *Total volume of oxygen produced in 8 minutes* ($cm^3$) | *Rate of oxygen production* ($cm^3$/minute) |
|---|---|---|
| P | 64 | 8 |
| Q | 96 | |

(i) Calculate the rate of oxygen production for Plant Q.

*Space for calculation*

____________________ $cm^3$/minute **1**

(ii) Calculate the ratio of oxygen produced by Plant P to that produced by Plant Q.

*Space for calculation*

________ : ________ **1**

DO NOT WRITE IN THIS MARGIN

Marks

**11. (continued)**

(*c*) The volume of oxygen produced was measured at time intervals of one minute. The results for Plant Q are shown in the line graph below.

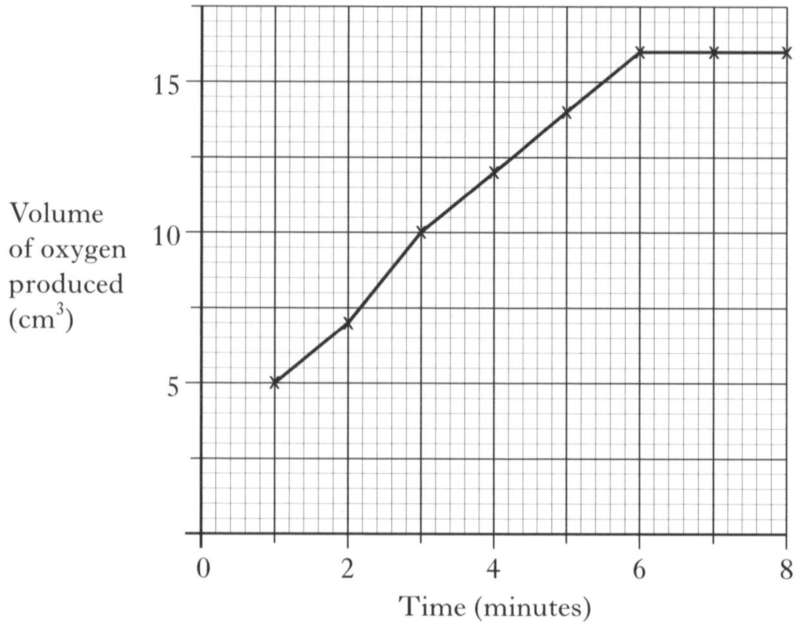


Describe what happens to the volume of oxygen produced per minute as the investigation proceeds.

______________________________________________

______________________________________________ **2**

(*d*) The diagram below shows the first stage in photosynthesis.

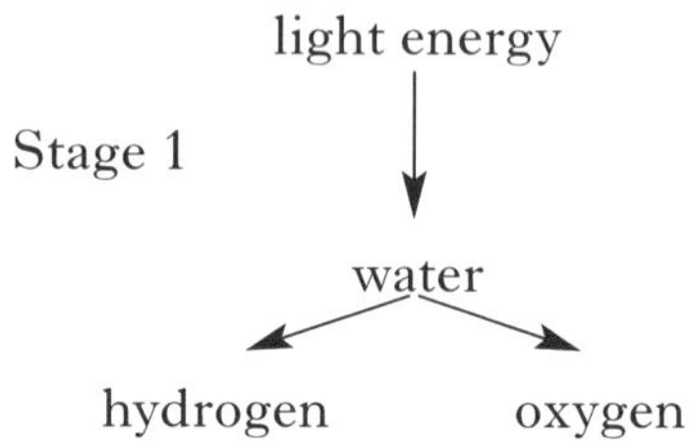


(i) Name the substance which captures the light energy needed at Stage 1.

______________________ **1**

(ii) The energy is used to split water molecules.
What name is given to this process?

______________________ **1**

(iii) The hydrogen then combines with carbon dioxide to form glucose.
Name this second stage in photosynthesis.

______________________ **1**

## SECTION C

*Marks*

**Answer BOTH questions 1 and 2 on the blank pages provided.**

**You may use labelled diagrams where appropriate.**

**1.** Answer **either** A **or** B.

A. The diagram below shows the nerve cells (neurones) involved in a reflex arc.

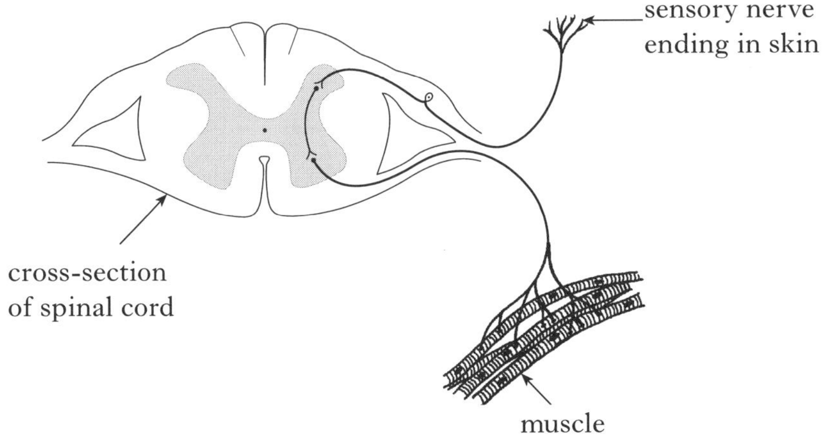


Describe the pathway of a nerve impulse through the reflex arc. **5**

**OR**

B. The diagram below shows a stage in the movement of food down the oesophagus.

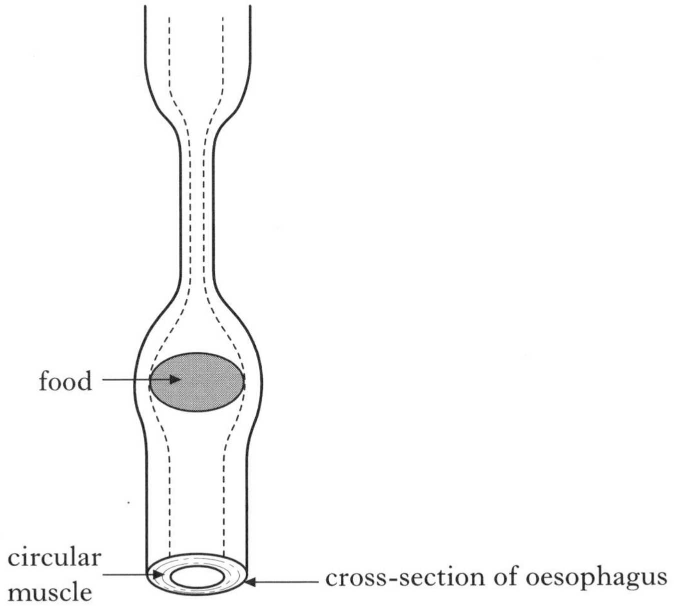


Name and describe the movement of the food through the oesophagus. **5**

DO NOT WRITE IN THIS MARGIN

*Marks*

**2.** Answer **either** A **or** B.

**You may use labelled diagrams where appropriate.**

A. Give an account of gamete formation in human females. **5**

**OR**

B. Describe, including examples, commercial and industrial uses of cells. **5**

[*END OF QUESTION PAPER*]

**[Turn over**

DO N
WRIT
TH
MAR

**SPACE FOR ANSWERS**

ADDITIONAL GRAPH PAPER FOR QUESTION 5(*c*)

# INTERMEDIATE 2 2001

FOR OFFICIAL USE

| | | | | | |
|---|---|---|---|---|---|
| | | | | | |

Total for Sections B and C

# X007/201

NATIONAL QUALIFICATIONS 2001

MONDAY, 21 MAY
9.00 AM – 11.00 AM

# BIOLOGY
## INTERMEDIATE 2

**Fill in these boxes and read what is printed below.**

Full name of centre

Town

Forename(s)

Surname

Date of birth
Day Month Year

Scottish candidate number

Number of seat

**SECTION A (25 marks)**

Instructions for completion of Section A are given on page two.

**SECTIONS B AND C (75 marks)**

1 (a) All questions should be attempted.

(b) It should be noted that in **Section C** questions 1 and 2 each contain a choice.

2 The questions may be answered in any order but all answers are to be written in the spaces provided in this answer book, and must be written clearly and legibly in ink.

3 Additional space for answers and rough work will be found at the end of the book. If further space is required, supplementary sheets may be obtained from the invigilator and should be inserted inside the **front** cover of this book.

4 The numbers of questions must be clearly inserted with any answers written in the additional space.

5 Rough work, if any should be necessary, should be written in this book and then scored through when the fair copy has been written.

6 Before leaving the examination room you must give this book to the invigilator. If you do not, you may lose all the marks for this paper.

SCOTTISH QUALIFICATIONS AUTHORITY
©

LIB X007/201 6/7470

**Read carefully**

1 Check that the answer sheet provided is for Biology Intermediate 2 (Section A).

2 Fill in the details required on the answer sheet.

3 In this section a question is answered by indicating the choice A, B, C or D by a stroke made in **ink** in the appropriate place in the answer sheet—see the sample question below.

4 For each question there is only **one** correct answer.

5 Rough working, if required, should be done only on this question paper, or on the rough working sheet provided—**not** on the answer sheet.

6 At the end of the examination the answer sheet for Section A **must** be placed inside the front cover of this answer book.

**Sample Question**

Which of the following lists all the elements that are present in every protein molecule?

A Carbon, oxygen, nitrogen

B Carbon, hydrogen, oxygen, nitrogen

C Carbon, hydrogen, oxygen, sulphur

D Carbon, hydrogen, oxygen

**The correct answer is B**—Carbon, hydrogen, oxygen, nitrogen. A **heavy** vertical line should be drawn joining the two dots in the appropriate box in the column headed **B** as shown **in the example on the answer sheet**.

If, after you have recorded your answer, you decide that you have made an error and wish to make a change, you should cancel the original answer and put a vertical stroke in the box you now consider to be correct. Thus, if you want to change an answer **D** to an answer **B**, your answer sheet would look like this:

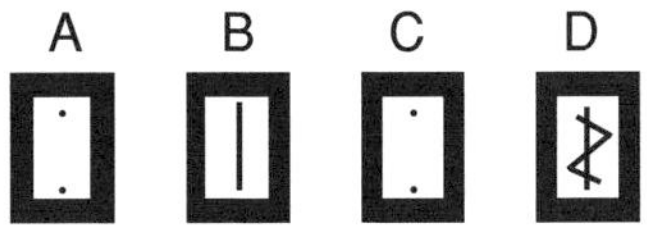


If you want to change back to an answer which has already been scored out, you should **enter a tick (✓)** to the RIGHT of the box of your choice, thus:

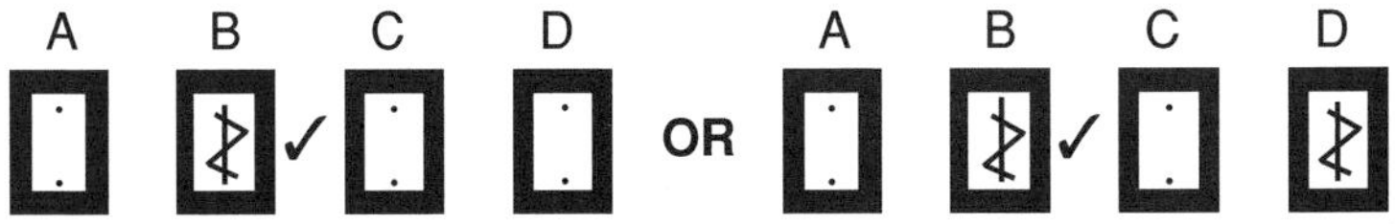

## SECTION A

**All questions in this Section should be attempted.**

**1.** Which term describes all the organisms living in the same area?

A Food web

B Ecosystem

C Population

D Community

**2.** Which term describes an animal that eats other animals in a food web?

A Prey

B Predator

C Producer

D Primary consumer

**3.** The diagram below shows a pyramid of biomass.

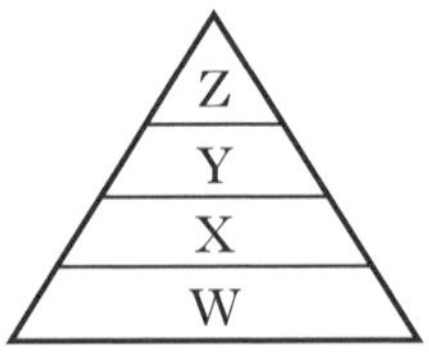


W represents the total mass of

A producers

B prey

C predators

D herbivores.

**Questions 4, 5 and 6** refer to the diagram and the information below.

A choice chamber was set up to investigate the response of woodlice to an environmental condition.

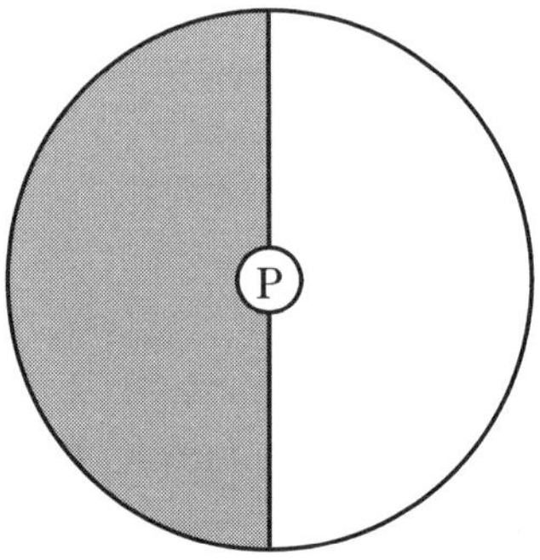


Thirty woodlice were placed in the choice chamber at point P.

The woodlice distribution was noted every 2 minutes during a 10 minute period.

The results are shown in the table below.

| | *Number of woodlice* | |
|---|---|---|
| *Time (minutes)* | *In the dark* | *In the light* |
| 2 | 12 | 18 |
| 4 | 13 | 17 |
| 6 | 15 | 15 |
| 8 | 19 | 11 |
| 10 | 27 | 3 |

**4.** The environmental condition being investigated is

A temperature

B number of woodlice

C light

D humidity.

**5.** The simple whole number ratio of woodlice found in the dark to those found in the light after two minutes was

A 2 : 3

B 3 : 2

C 6 : 9

D 12 : 18.

**6.** A possible conclusion from this investigation is

A woodlice are more likely to be found in the light

B woodlice are more likely to be found in the dark

C woodlice cannot detect light

D woodlice show no difference in their response to light and dark.

**7.** What must be present in leaf cells for photosynthesis to take place?

A Carbon dioxide and water

B Oxygen and water

C Carbon dioxide and oxygen

D Oxygen and hydrogen

**8.** Products of the photolysis stage of photosynthesis are

A glucose and hydrogen

B carbon dioxide and hydrogen

C water and oxygen

D hydrogen and oxygen.

**9.** The diagram below shows the carbon fixation stage of photosynthesis.

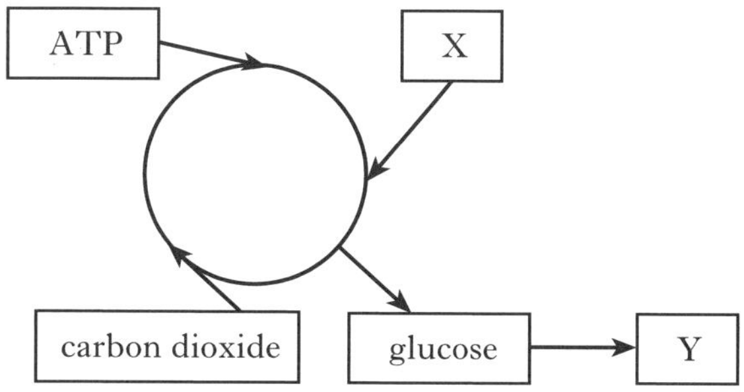


Which line in the table correctly identifies X and Y?

| | X | Y |
|---|---|---|
| A | hydrogen | starch |
| B | starch | ADP |
| C | starch | oxygen |
| D | water | starch |

**10.** The graph below shows the changing pH of a sample of milk over a seven day period.

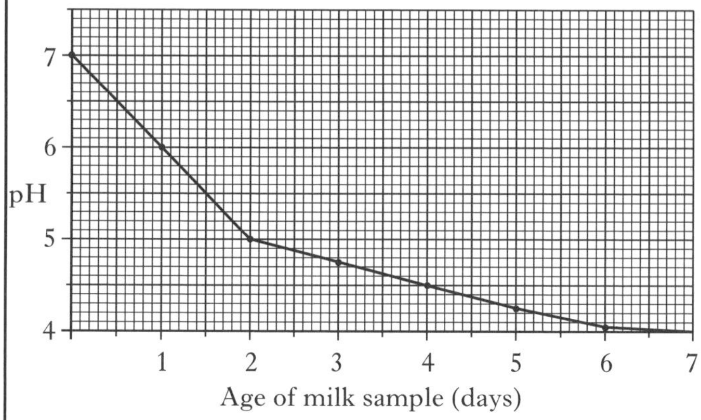


The changes in pH are due to

A lactic acid in the milk destroying the bacteria

B enzymes in the milk being denatured

C bacteria in the milk causing the production of lactic acid

D bacteria in the milk producing carbon dioxide.

**Questions 11 and 12** refer to the diagram below which shows a section through a mammalian heart.

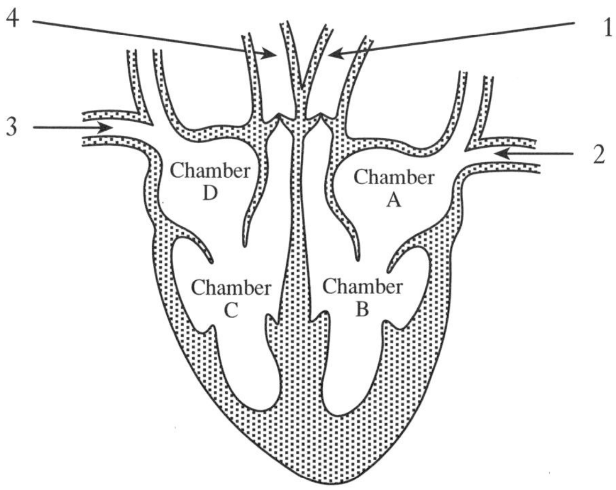


**11.** Which arrow identifies the vena cava?

A 1

B 2

C 3

D 4

**12.** Which heart chamber pumps blood to the lungs?

**13.** Which letter correctly identifies the location of the sensory strip of the cerebrum?

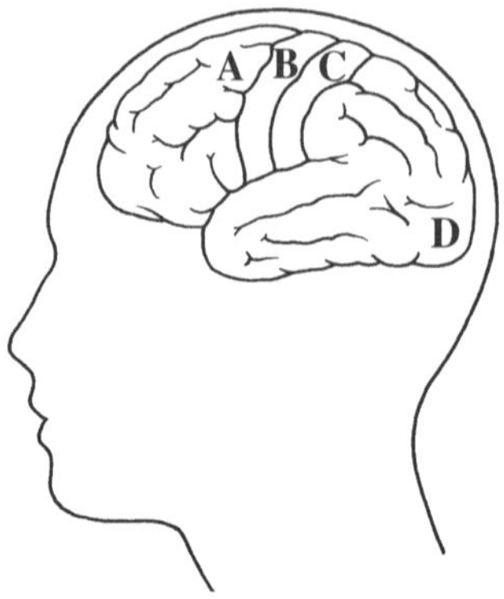


**14.** The diagram below shows a site of gas exchange in the lungs.

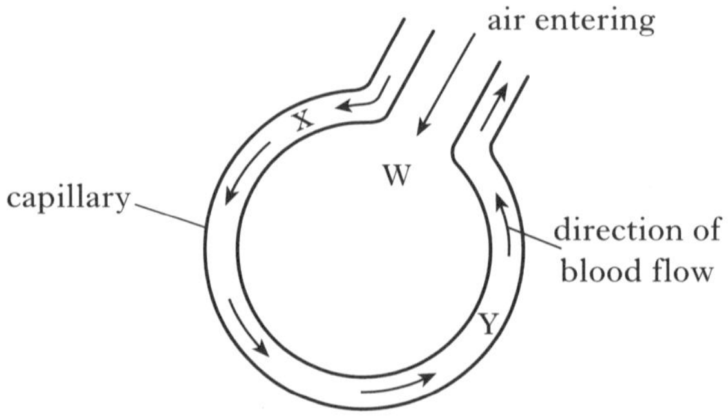


Which line in the table shows the correct relative concentrations of oxygen?

| | *Concentration of oxygen* | | |
|---|---|---|---|
| | *at W* | *at X* | *at Y* |
| A | high | low | high |
| B | low | high | low |
| C | low | high | high |
| D | high | high | low |

**Questions 15 and 16** refer to the graph below.

The graph shows the percentage saturation of haemoglobin at different oxygen concentrations.

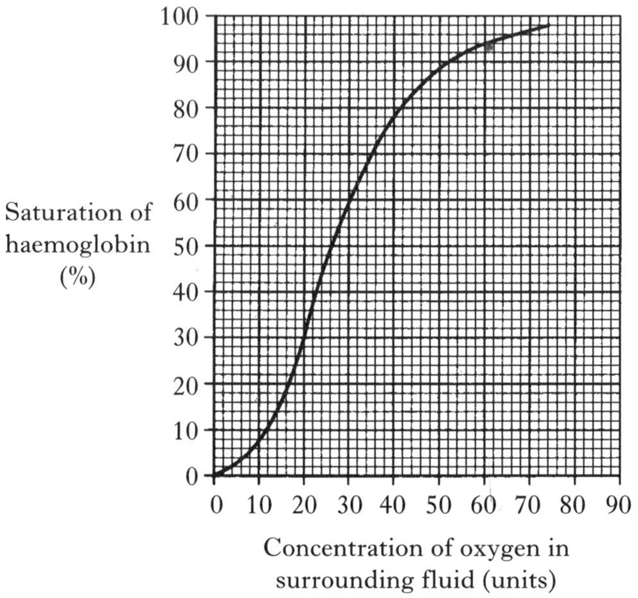


**15.** What is the percentage saturation of haemoglobin with oxygen when the oxygen concentration of the surroundings is 60 units?

A 30

B 90

C 92

D 94

**16.** What is the increase in percentage saturation of haemoglobin with oxygen as the oxygen concentration of the surroundings increases from 20 to 40 units?

A 20

B 30

C 48

D 78

**17.** Digestion takes place in animals

A and allows insoluble molecules to pass directly through the wall of the small intestine

B as enzymes cannot act on insoluble molecules

C and makes insoluble molecules soluble to allow absorption

D and allows food to be passed along the gut by peristalsis.

**18.** The hepatic portal vein transports

A glucose from the large intestine to the liver

B amino acids from the small intestine to the liver

C fats from the lacteal to the liver

D urea from the kidneys to the liver.

**19.** Which substances are normally excreted in urine?

A Protein and urea

B Urea and salts

C Glucose and salts

D Protein and salts

**[Turn over**

**20.** The table below shows water gained and lost by the body over a 24 hour period.

| *Method of water gain* | *Volume of water gained* (cm$^3$) | *Method of water loss* | *Volume of water lost* (cm$^3$) |
|---|---|---|---|
| food | 800 | exhaled breath | |
| drink | 1000 | sweating | 500 |
| metabolic water | 350 | urine | 1250 |
| | | faeces | 100 |

What volume of water is lost in exhaled breath?

A 100 cm$^3$

B 200 cm$^3$

C 300 cm$^3$

D 500 cm$^3$

**21.** After running a race an athlete experienced muscle fatigue.

Which of the following increased in the muscles?

A Glucose

B Oxygen

C ATP

D Lactic acid

**22.** During aerobic respiration in muscle cells oxygen will combine with

A hydrogen to form water

B pyruvic acid to form lactic acid

C pyruvic acid to form ethanol

D glucose to form pyruvic acid.

**23.** Which of the following is a correct description of a chromosome?

A A chain of DNA bases

B A chain of RNA bases

C A chain of amino acids

D A chain of sugar molecules

**24.** If an inherited characteristic is controlled by alleles of more than one gene, then the type of inheritance is called

A true breeding

B polygenic

C co-dominant

D monohybrid.

**25.** The diagram below represents the transmission of sex determining chromosomes from parents to offspring.

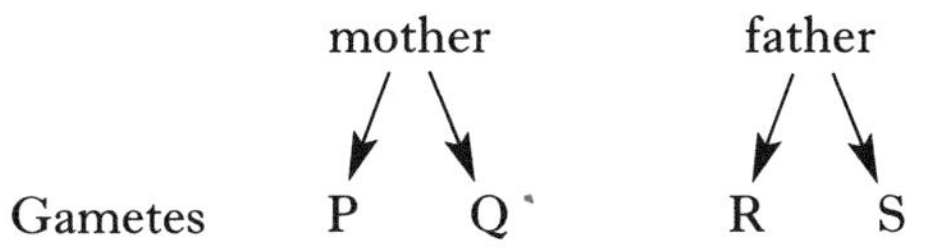


Which line in the table below correctly identifies the sex chromosomes for the gametes P, Q, R and S?

| | *Gamete P* | *Gamete Q* | *Gamete R* | *Gamete S* |
|---|---|---|---|---|
| A | XX | XX | XY | XY |
| B | X | X | X | Y |
| C | XX | XY | XX | XY |
| D | X | Y | X | Y |

**Candidates are reminded that the answer sheet for Section A MUST be placed <u>inside</u> the front cover of this answer book.**

DO NOT WRITE IN THIS MARGIN

## SECTION B

**All questions in this section should be attempted.**

*Marks*

**1.** The diagrams below show sections of three different cell types.

They are not drawn to the same scale.

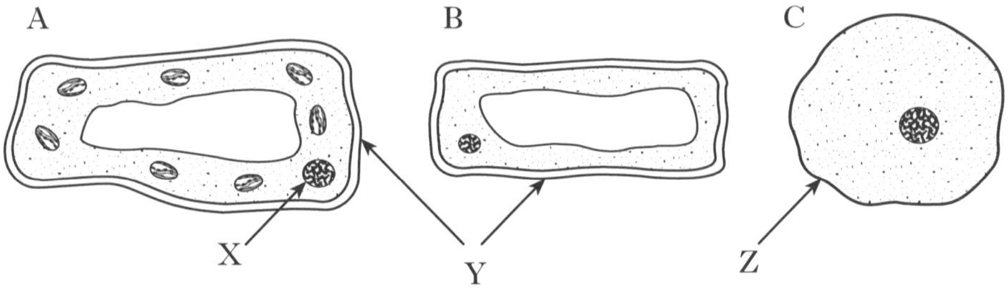


(*a*) (i) Complete the table below to show the name and function of the parts labelled X, Y and Z.

| *Part of cell* | *Name* | *Function* |
|---|---|---|
| X | | |
| Y | | |
| Z | | |

**2**

(ii) Cells A and B are plant cells and cell C is an animal cell.

Describe **two** features, shown in the diagrams, that support this statement.

______________________________________________

______________________________________________ **2**

(*b*) Name a substance produced by cell type A that can be used by cell types B and C.

______________________________ **1**

**[Turn over**

DO NOT WRITE IN THIS MARGIN

*Marks*

**2.** (*a*) An investigation into the effect of temperature on anaerobic respiration in yeast was carried out.

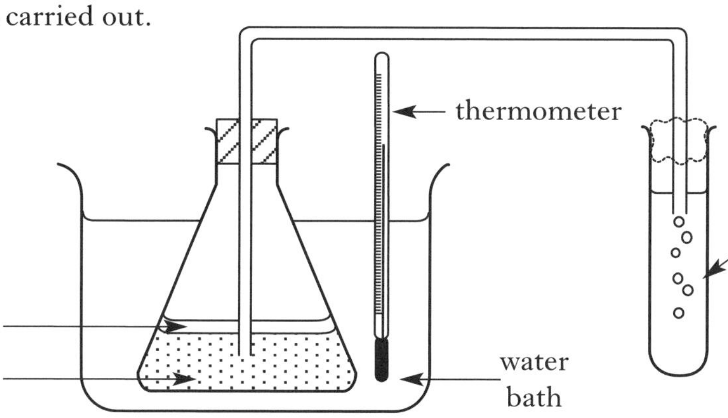


1. A glucose solution was boiled and cooled and poured into a conical flask.
2. A yeast suspension was added to the glucose solution.
3. Oil was poured over the surface of the liquid.
4. The number of bubbles of carbon dioxide produced in one minute was counted.
5. The procedure was repeated at a range of temperatures.

(i) In this investigation temperature was the only variable altered.

State **two** variables that should be kept constant when setting up this investigation.

1 ____________________

2 ____________________ **2**

(ii) Explain the purpose of the layer of oil.

____________________ **1**

(iii) The results are shown in the table below.

| *Temperature* (°C) | *Bubbles of carbon dioxide* (number/minute) |
|---|---|
| 4 | 0 |
| 20 | 3 |
| 35 | 6 |
| 45 | 22 |
| 50 | 20 |
| 70 | 0 |

DO NOT WRITE IN THIS MARGIN

Marks

**2.** **(*a*)** **(continued)**

Present the results in a suitable format on the grid below.
(Additional graph paper, if required, will be found on page 28.)

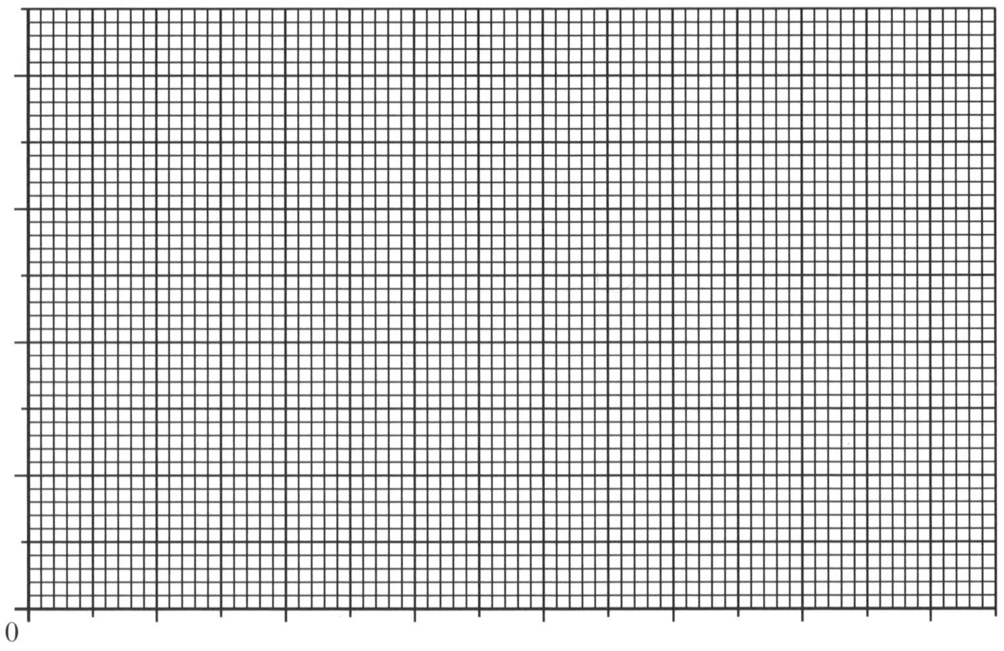


Temperature (°C) **3**

(iv) From the results, describe the effect of temperature on anaerobic respiration in yeast.

________________________________________________

________________________________________________ **2**

(v) Suggest **one** way in which the reliability of the results could be improved.

________________________________________________ **1**

(vi) In addition to carbon dioxide, what will be produced in the flask during the investigation?

_________________________ **1**

(vii) Explain why no carbon dioxide is produced when the temperature is 70 °C.

________________________________________________ **1**

(*b*) Yeast is a micro-organism used in the production of bread.

Name **one** other type of micro-organism and an associated product.

____________________ used to produce ____________________. **1**

DO NOT WRITE IN THIS MARGIN

Marks

**3.** The diagram below shows part of the human circulatory system.

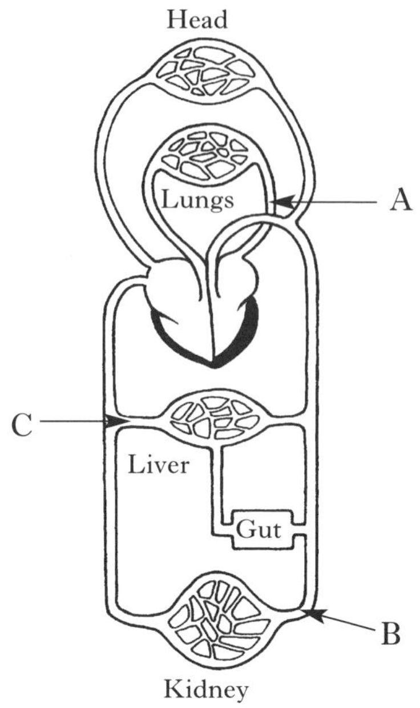


(*a*) Name the blood vessels labelled A, B and C in the diagram.

A ______________________

B ______________________

C ______________________ **3**

(*b*) The diagram below shows a cross section through an artery.

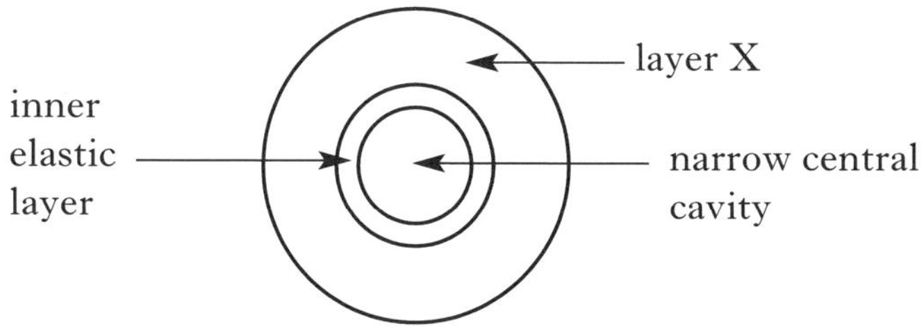


(i) Describe layer X.

______________________________________________ **1**

(ii) Describe how the structure of layer X is related to its function.

______________________________________________ **1**

(iii) The pulse beat can be felt in an artery.

What causes the pulse beat?

______________________________________________ **1**

DO NOT WRITE IN THIS MARGIN

*Marks*

**4.** (*a*) (i) Describe **two** features of the lungs which make them efficient gas exchange surfaces.

1 ________________________________________

2 ________________________________________ **2**

(ii) Name the structures in the lungs through which oxygen diffuses from the air into the blood capillaries.

________________________________________ **1**

(*b*) The table below shows the rates of oxygen intake and energy release during various activities.

| *Activity* | *Rate of oxygen intake* ($cm^3$/second) | *Rate of energy release* (joules/second) |
|---|---|---|
| Resting | 3·5 | 70 |
| Playing golf | 20 | 400 |
| Playing tennis | 25 | 500 |
| Playing football | 30 | 600 |

Describe the relationship between oxygen intake and energy release.

______________________________________________________________ **1**

**[Turn over**

DO NOT WRITE IN THIS MARGIN

*Marks*

**5.** (*a*) Some information on digestion and absorption of the main food groups is given in Table 1 below.

Table 1

| *Food group* | *Product(s) of digestion* | *Use after absorption* |
|---|---|---|
| Carbohydrate | | Energy production |
| Protein | | Making new proteins for growth and repair |
| Fat | Fatty acids and glycerol | |

(i) Complete the table to show the products of digestion and their uses after absorption. **2**

(ii) Name the chemical elements present in fat molecules.

______________________________ **1**

(*b*) The nutritional information for 100 g of a breakfast cereal is shown in Table 2 below.

Table 2

| | *Each 100g of cereal provides* |
|---|---|
| Energy | 1440 kJ |
| Protein | 11·2 g |
| Carbohydrate | 67·6 g |
| Fat | 2·7 g |
| Vitamins | 18·0 mg |
| Fibre | 10·5 g |

DO NOT WRITE IN THIS MARGIN

*Marks*

**5. (*b*) (continued)**

(i) The total daily energy requirement for a sixteen year old girl is 9600 kJ.

Calculate the percentage of her daily total energy requirement that would be provided by a 50 g portion of breakfast cereal each day.

*Space for calculation*

________________ % **1**

(ii) Which food group is missing from Table 2?

______________________________ **1**

**[Turn over**

*Marks*

**6.** (*a*) Pepsin is an enzyme that breaks down protein.

Photographic film that has been exposed and developed has a black coating that is held on by a protein layer.

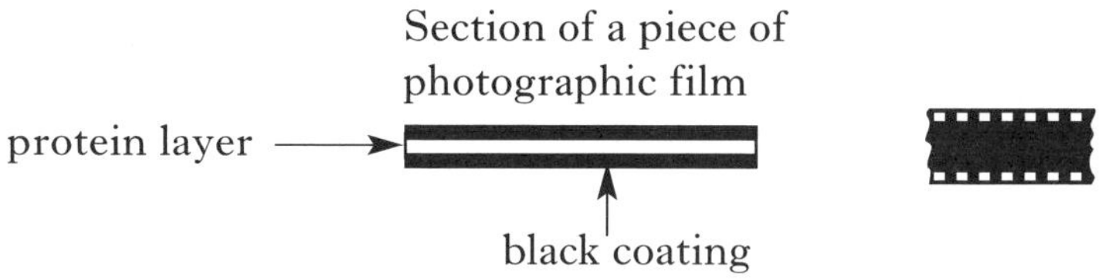


The diagram below shows the results of an investigation into the activity of the enzyme pepsin.

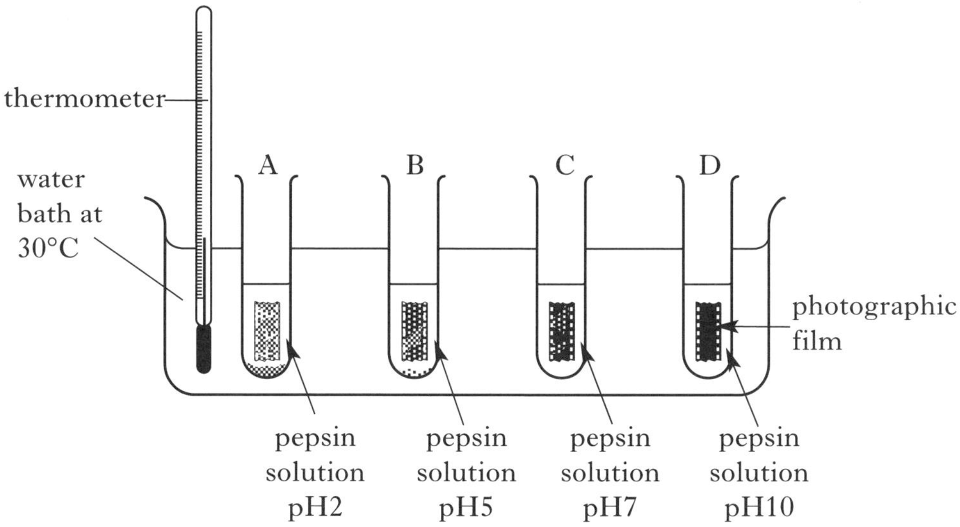


(i) Name the variable studied in this investigation.

_______________________________ **1**

(ii) Explain why most protein was broken down in Tube A.

_______________________________ **1**

(iii) Describe suitable controls to show that the enzyme is causing the observed effects.

_______________________________

_______________________________ **1**

(*b*) Pepsin is the enzyme produced by secretory cells in the stomach.

Describe the function of the mucus also produced in the stomach.

_______________________________ **1**

DO NOT WRITE IN THIS MARGIN

*Marks*

**7.** (*a*) Groups of students carried out an investigation into the effects of competition.

Trays containing seeds were set up as shown below.

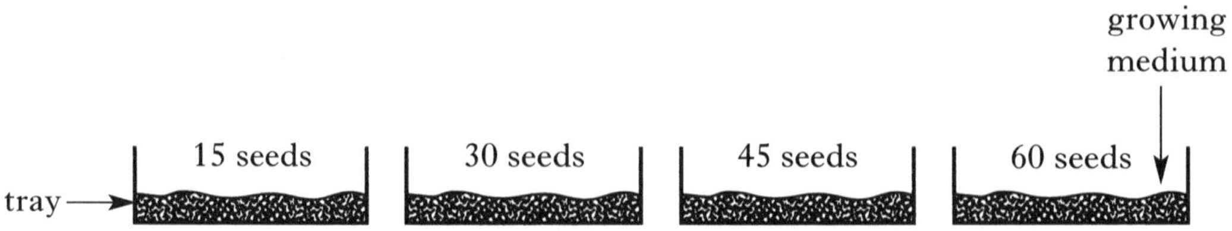


The trays were watered regularly to allow germination to take place.

After several days the seedlings were observed and the number with healthy green leaves was noted.

The results are shown in the table below.

| *Number of seeds in each tray* | *Number of seedlings with healthy green leaves* | *Percentage of seedlings with healthy green leaves* |
|---|---|---|
| 15 | 12 | 80 |
| 30 | 18 | 60 |
| 45 | 23 | 51 |
| 60 | 24 | 40 |

(i) Predict the percentage of seedlings with healthy green leaves if 75 seeds were sown in a seed tray.

______________________________ **1**

(ii) State **two** factors for which the seedlings could be competing in this investigation.

1 ______________________________

2 ______________________________ **1**

**[Turn over**

*Marks*

**7. (continued)**

(*b*) A horticulturist grew a crop of peas in a polythene tunnel.

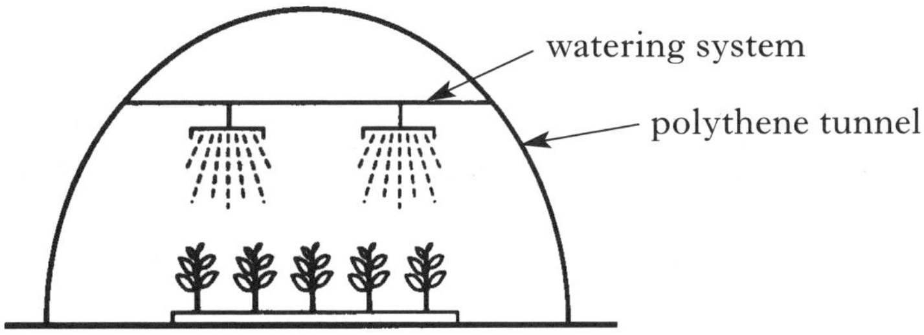


State **two** conditions that could limit the rate of photosynthesis in the pea plants.

1 ____________________

2 ____________________ **2**

(*c*) The graph below shows the mass of sugar in the leaves and the concentration of carbon dioxide just above the leaves of pea plants at different times of the day.

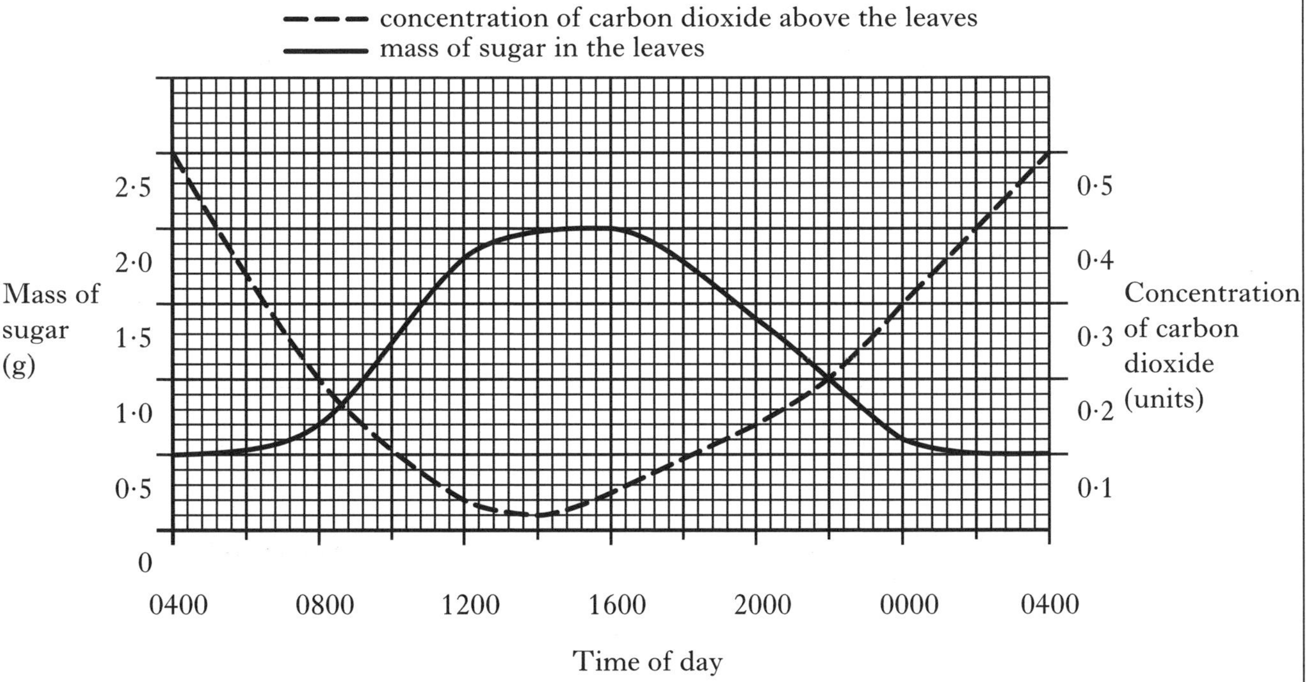


(i) For how many hours did the carbon dioxide concentration decrease?

__________ hours **1**

DO NOT WRITE IN THIS MARGIN

*Marks*

**7. (*c*) (continued)**

(ii) Explain this decrease in carbon dioxide concentration.

______________________________________________

______________________________________________ **1**

(iii) Explain why the mass of sugar in the leaves is at its maximum at 1600.

______________________________________________

______________________________________________ **1**

(iv) Calculate the **percentage increase** in sugar in the leaves between 0400 and 1600.

*Space for calculation*

__________ % **1**

(v) Give **two** reasons why the mass of sugar decreases between 2000 and 0000.

1 ______________________________________________

2 ______________________________________________ **2**

**[Turn over**

DO NOT WRITE IN THIS MARGIN

*Marks*

**8.** (*a*) Name the male gametes and their site of production in a flower.

Male gametes ______________________________

Site of production ______________________________ **2**

(*b*) Tomato plants were used in an experimental monohybrid cross.

The parental phenotypes were cut leaf and potato leaf as shown in the diagrams below.

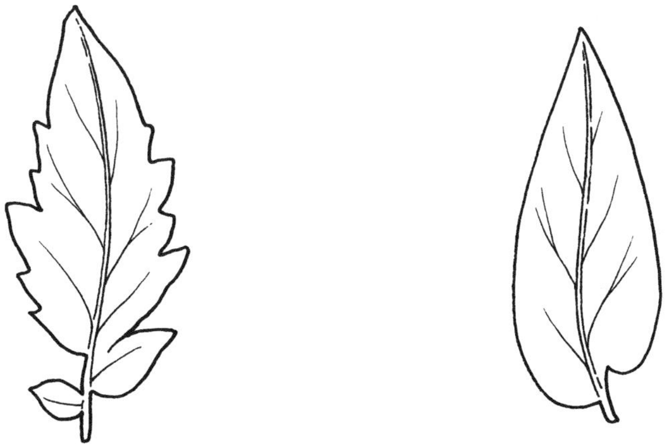


The parent plants were both true breeding.

The $F_1$ plants were self-pollinated.

The $F_2$ generation contained 80 plants with the cut leaf genotype and 20 plants with the potato leaf genotype.

(i) Explain what is meant by the term true breeding.

________________________________________________ **1**

(ii) State which characteristic is dominant and give a reason.

Dominant characteristic ________________________

Reason __________________________________________ **1**

DO NOT WRITE IN THIS MARGIN

*Marks*

**8. (*b*) (continued)**

(iii) The results obtained in the $F_2$ generation differ from the expected results.

There were 100 plants in the $F_2$ generation.

Calculate the number of plants which would have been expected to have the cut leaf phenotype in the $F_2$ generation.

*Space for calculation*

__________ plants **1**

(iv) Suggest one reason why the results obtained differ from the expected results.

________________________________________ **1**

**[Turn over**

*Marks*

**9.** (*a*) The diagram below shows part of a food web from a moorland ecosystem.

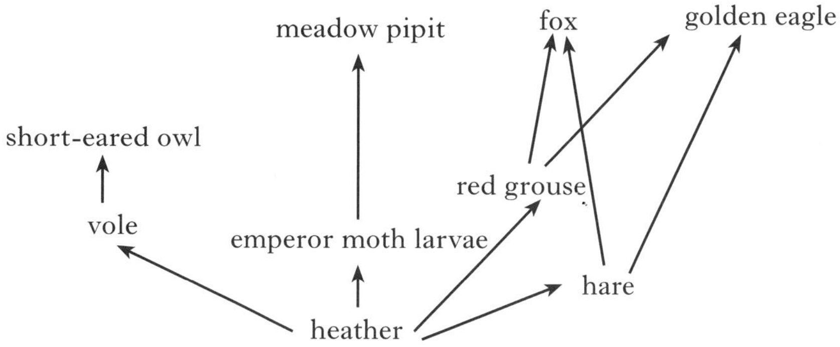


(i) Write each organism from the food web in the correct column in the table below.

| *Producer* | *Primary consumer* | *Secondary consumer* |
|---|---|---|
| | | |

2

(ii) Describe **one** possible effect on the food web of a large increase in the grouse population.

________________________________________ 1

(iii) Human activities can affect the biodiversity of an ecosystem.

Explain the term "biodiversity".

________________________________________ 1

(*b*) Give one characteristic of a **stable** ecosystem.

________________________________________ 1

DO NOT WRITE IN THIS MARGIN

*Marks*

**10.** The diagram below shows a genetically-engineered bacterial cell.

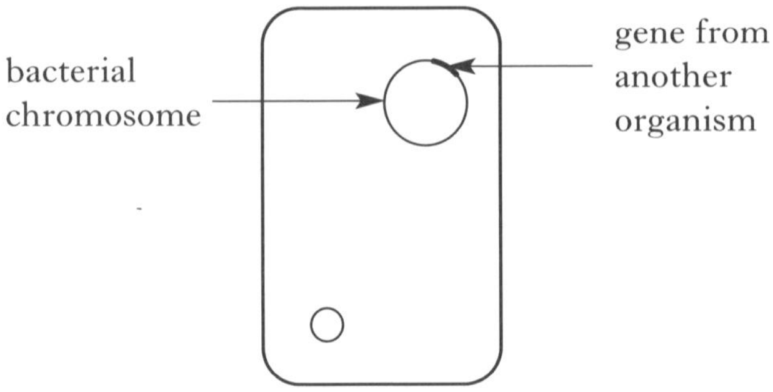


(*a*) Name the type of molecule found in a bacterial chromosome.

______________________________ **1**

(*b*) The bacterium was genetically engineered to produce a particular substance.

Name one example of a substance which can be produced in this way and describe its use.

Substance ______________________________

Use ______________________________

______________________________ **1**

(*c*) Genetic engineering can produce new genotypes to provide better organisms for particular functions.

Give one advantage and one disadvantage of genetic engineering compared with selective breeding.

Advantage ______________________________

______________________________ **1**

Disadvantage ______________________________

______________________________ **1**

**[Turn over**

*Marks*

**11.** (*a*) In 1994 a survey of habitats was carried out in West Lothian.

The table below shows the range of types of habitat in an area of 50 000 hectares.

The information was used to monitor the success of a biodiversity enhancement programme.

| *Type of habitat* | *Area* (hectares) | *Percentage cover* |
|---|---|---|
| woodland and scrub | 7 000 | 14·0 |
| grassland | 18 000 | 36·0 |
| tall herb and fen | 300 | 0·6 |
| heathland | 1 500 | 3·0 |
| peatland | 2 000 | 4·0 |
| open water | 500 | |
| cultivated land | 13 500 | 27·0 |
| unsurveyed urban areas | 6 600 | 13·2 |
| others | 600 | 1·2 |

(i) Complete the bar graph below to illustrate some of the information in the table.
(Additional graph paper, if required, will be found on page 28.)

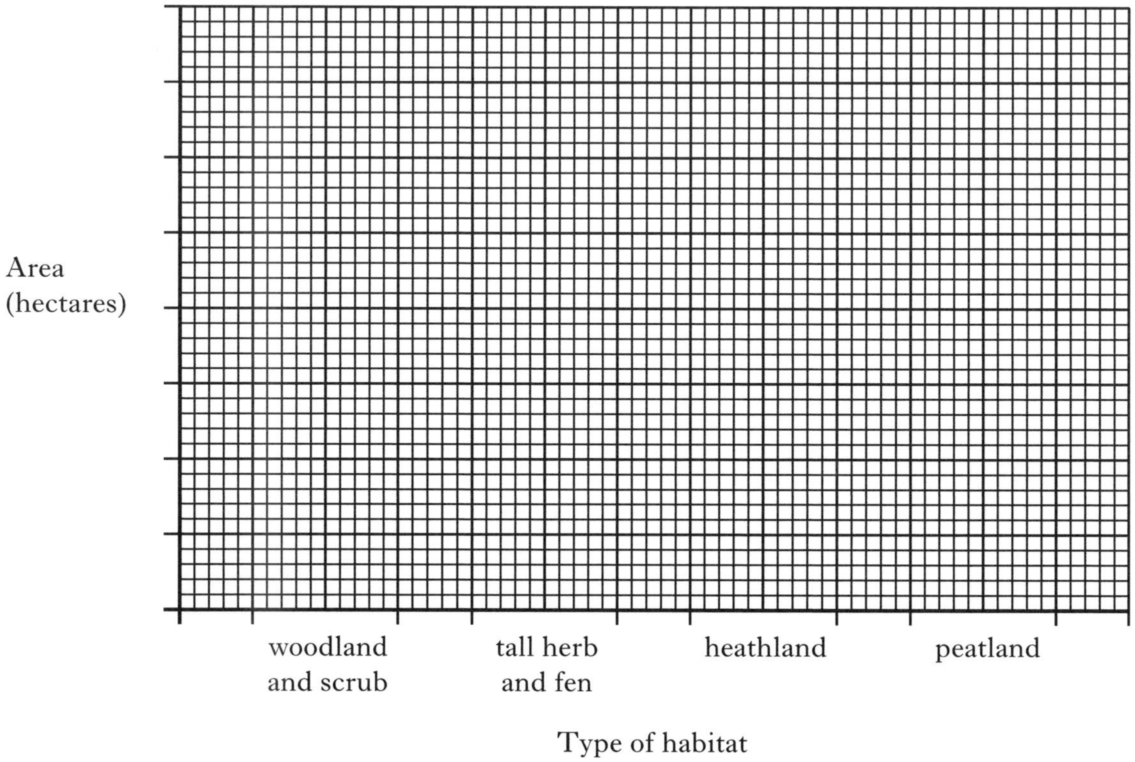


2

DO NOT WRITE IN THIS MARGIN

*Marks*

**11. (*a*) (continued)**

(ii) Calculate the percentage of the area which is open water.

*Space for calculation*

______ % **1**

(*b*) Name **one** human activity which could affect biodiversity in the open water habitat.

______________________________ **1**

**[Turn over**

DO NOT WRITE IN THIS MARGIN

Marks

## SECTION C

**Both questions in this section should be attempted.**

Note that each question contains a choice.

**Questions 1 and 2 should be attempted on the blank pages which follow.**

**Supplementary sheets, if required, may be obtained from the invigilator.**

**Labelled diagrams may be included where appropriate.**

**In question 1, ONE mark is available for coherence.**

1. Answer **either** A **or** B.

A. The diagram below shows the appearance of human red blood cells in an isotonic solution.

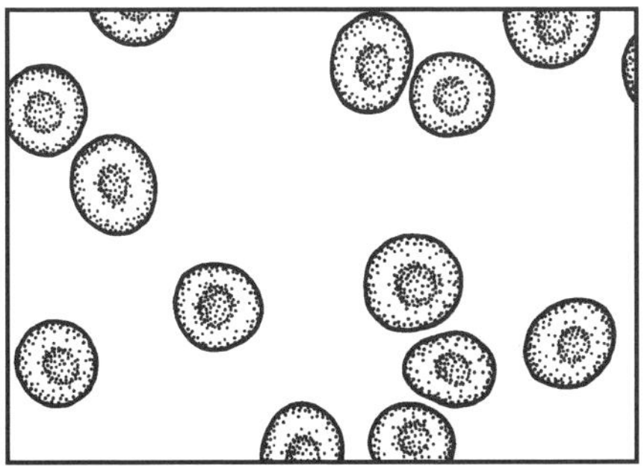

Describe and explain the events which would take place if these red blood cells were transferred to pure water. **5**

**OR**

B. The diagram below represents an amylase molecule.

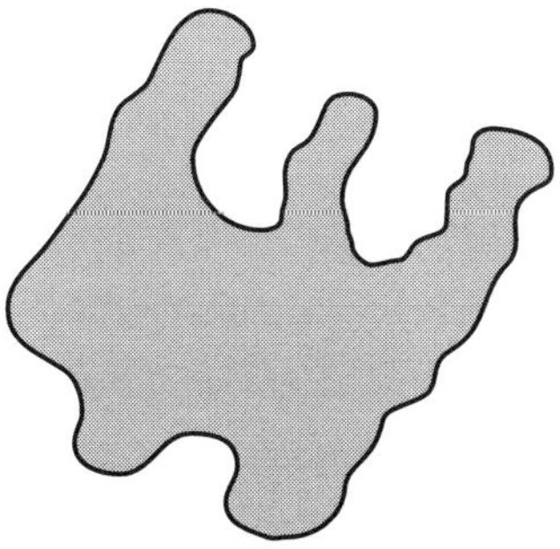

Describe and explain the events that take place when the enzyme is added to a starch suspension. **5**

**Question 2 is on *page twenty-six*.**

DO NOT WRITE IN THIS MARGIN

*Marks*

**SPACE FOR ANSWER TO QUESTION 1**

**[Turn over for Question 2 on *page twenty-six***

DO NOT WRITE IN THIS MARGIN

*Marks*

**2.** Answer **either** A **or** B.

**Labelled diagrams may be included where appropriate.**

A. Describe the functions of macrophages and lymphocytes in defence. **5**

**OR**

B. Describe the functions of the hypothalamus and blood vessels in temperature regulation. **5**

[*END OF QUESTION PAPER*]

DO NOT WRITE IN THIS MARGIN

**SPACE FOR ANSWER TO QUESTION 2**

**SPACE FOR ANSWERS**

ADDITIONAL GRAPH PAPER FOR QUESTION 2(*a*)

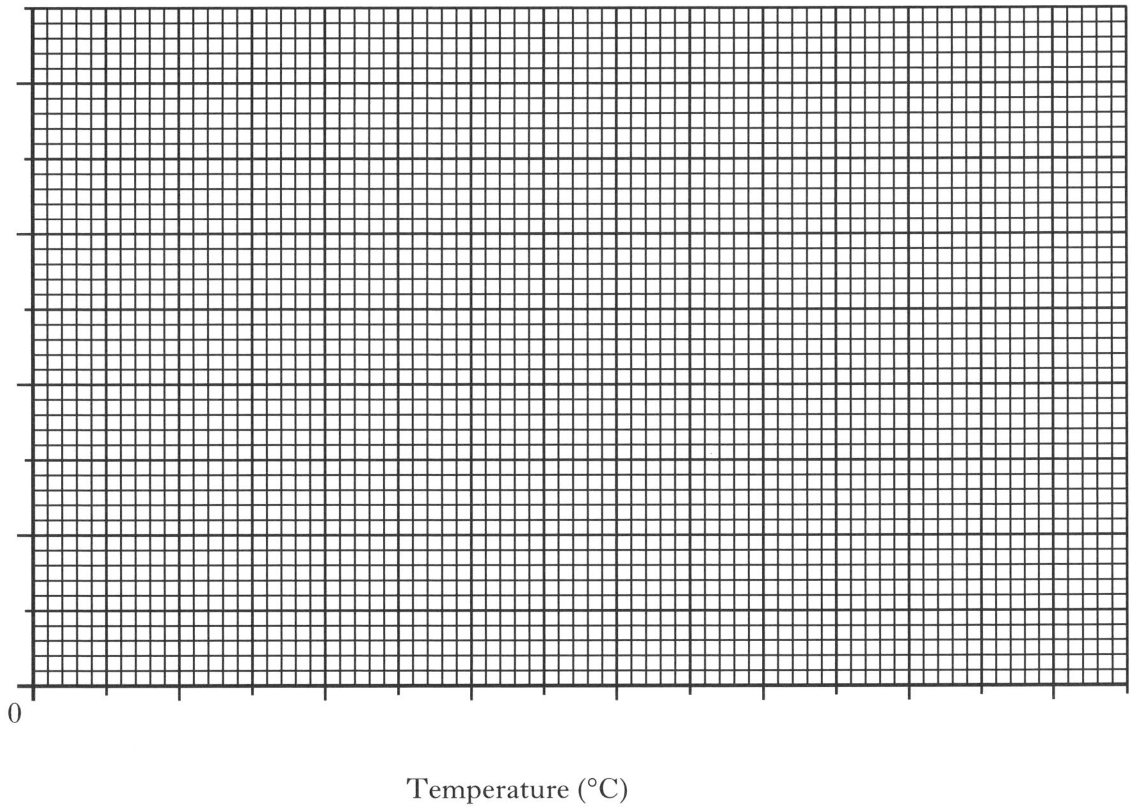


ADDITIONAL GRAPH PAPER FOR QUESTION 11(*a*)(i)

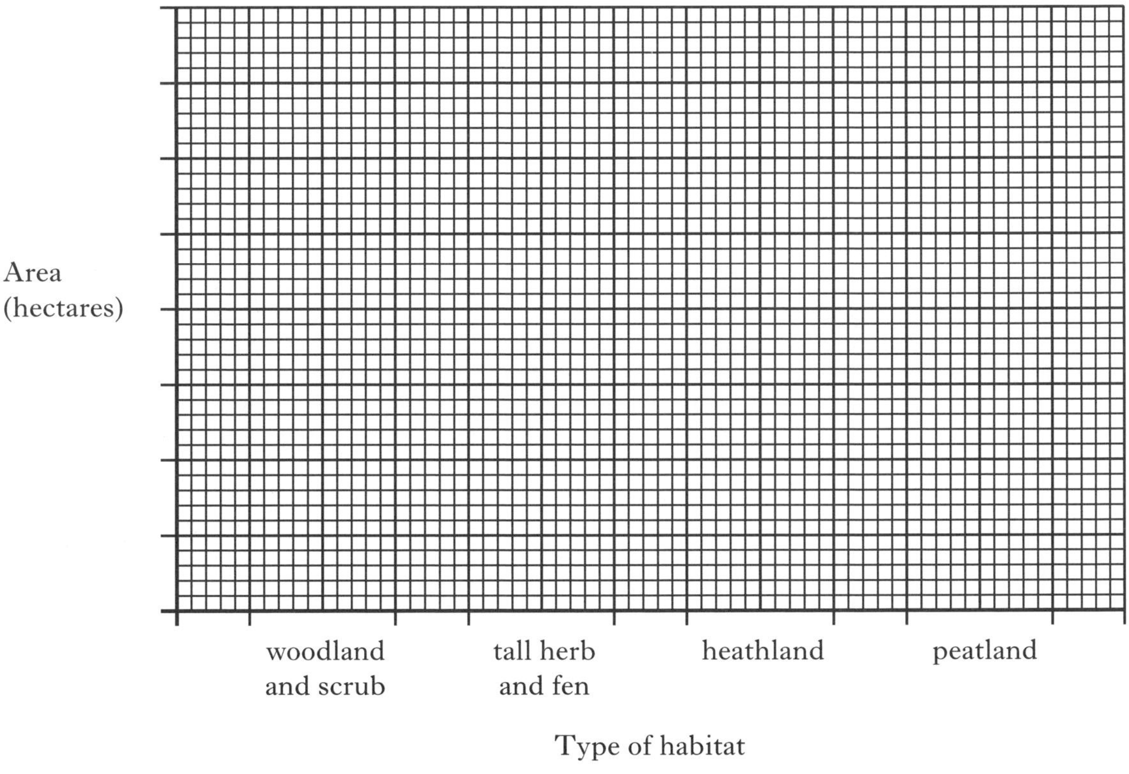

INTERMEDIATE 2 2002

FOR OFFICIAL USE

| | | | | | |
|---|---|---|---|---|---|
| | | | | | |

Total for Sections B and C

# X007/201

NATIONAL QUALIFICATIONS 2002

FRIDAY, 31 MAY
1.00 PM – 3.00 PM

# BIOLOGY
## INTERMEDIATE 2

**Fill in these boxes and read what is printed below.**

Full name of centre

Town

Forename(s)

Surname

Date of birth
Day Month Year

Scottish candidate number

Number of seat

**SECTION A (25 marks)**

Instructions for completion of Section A are given on page two.

**SECTIONS B AND C (75 marks)**

1 (a) All questions should be attempted.

(b) It should be noted that in **Section C** questions 1 and 2 each contain a choice.

2 The questions may be answered in any order but all answers are to be written in the spaces provided in this answer book, and must be written clearly and legibly in ink.

3 Additional space for answers and rough work will be found at the end of the book. If further space is required, supplementary sheets may be obtained from the invigilator and should be inserted inside the **front** cover of this book.

4 The numbers of questions must be clearly inserted with any answers written in the additional space.

5 Rough work, if any should be necessary, should be written in this book and then scored through when the fair copy has been written.

6 Before leaving the examination room you must give this book to the invigilator. If you do not, you may lose all the marks for this paper.

SCOTTISH QUALIFICATIONS AUTHORITY

**Read carefully**

1 Check that the answer sheet provided is for Biology Intermediate 2 (Section A).

2 Fill in the details required on the answer sheet.

3 In this section a question is answered by indicating the choice A, B, C or D by a stroke made in **ink** in the appropriate place in the answer sheet—see the sample question below.

4 For each question there is only **one** correct answer.

5 Rough working, if required, should be done only on this question paper, or on the rough working sheet provided—**not** on the answer sheet.

6 At the end of the examination the answer sheet for Section A **must** be placed inside the front cover of this answer book.

**Sample Question**

Which of the following lists all the elements that are present in every protein molecule?

A Carbon, oxygen, nitrogen

B Carbon, hydrogen, oxygen, nitrogen

C Carbon, hydrogen, oxygen, sulphur

D Carbon, hydrogen, oxygen

**The correct answer is B**—Carbon, hydrogen, oxygen, nitrogen. A **heavy** vertical line should be drawn joining the two dots in the appropriate box in the column headed **B** as shown **in the example on the answer sheet**.

If, after you have recorded your answer, you decide that you have made an error and wish to make a change, you should cancel the original answer and put a vertical stroke in the box you now consider to be correct. Thus, if you want to change an answer **D** to an answer **B**, your answer sheet would look like this:

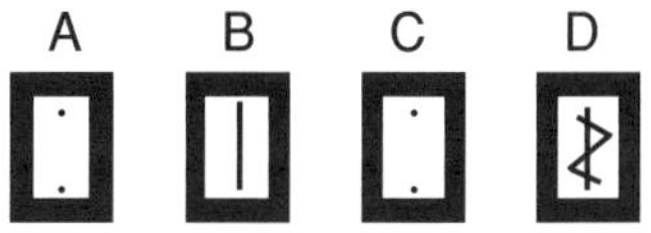


If you want to change back to an answer which has already been scored out, you should **enter a tick (✓)** to the RIGHT of the box of your choice, thus:

## SECTION A

**All questions in this Section should be attempted.**

**Questions 1 and 2** refer to the diagram of the digestive system below.

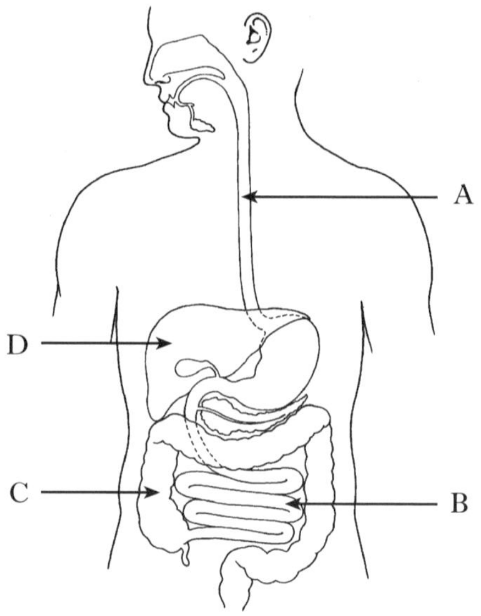


**1.** Which labelled arrow identifies the small intestine?

**2.** Which labelled arrow identifies where water is absorbed?

**3.** The diagram below shows some structures in a villus.

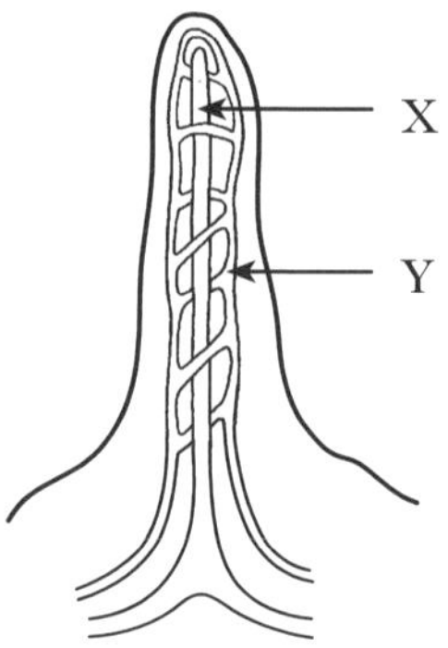


Which line in the table below correctly identifies the products of digestion which pass into structures X and Y?

| | X | Y |
|---|---|---|
| A | glucose | amino acids |
| B | glycerol | fatty acids |
| C | amino acids | glycogen |
| D | fatty acids | glucose |

**4.** The key below can be used to identify four components of blood, P, Q, R and S.

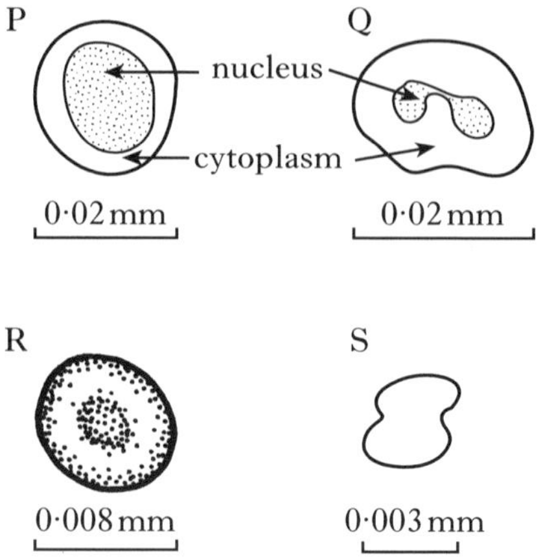


1. Nucleus present.............................. go to 2
   Nucleus absent ............................... go to 3
2. Large volume of cytoplasm present .. macrophage
   Small volume of cytoplasm present .. lymphocyte
3. Diameter greater than 0·005 mm ...... red blood cell
   Diameter less than 0·005mm ........... platelet

Which line in the table correctly identifies the blood components?

| | P | Q | R | S |
|---|---|---|---|---|
| A | lymphocyte | red blood cell | platelet | macrophage |
| B | macrophage | lymphocyte | red blood cell | platelet |
| C | platelet | macrophage | red blood cell | lymphocyte |
| D | lymphocyte | macrophage | red blood cell | platelet |

**[Turn over**

**5.** The diagrams below show stages in the process of phagocytosis as carried out by a macrophage.

1. The bacterium is trapped in the vacuole.

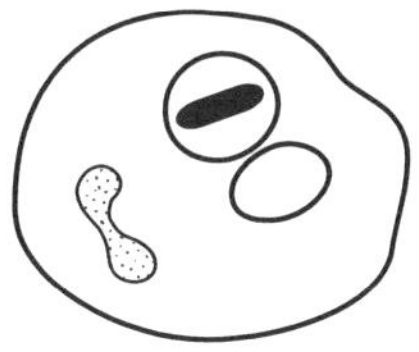

2. A vacuole forms in the macrophage.

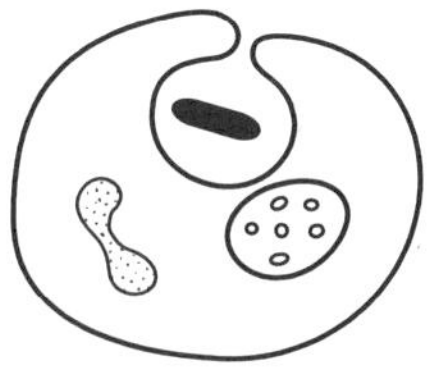

3. The bacterium is digested by enzymes.

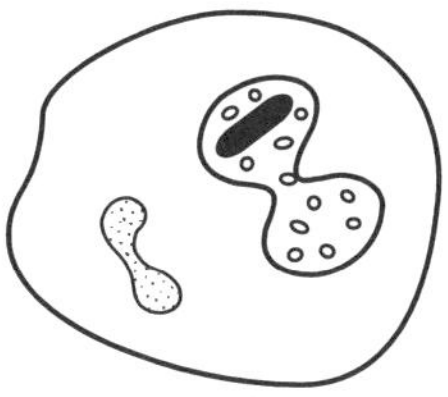

4. The macrophage engulfs the bacterium.

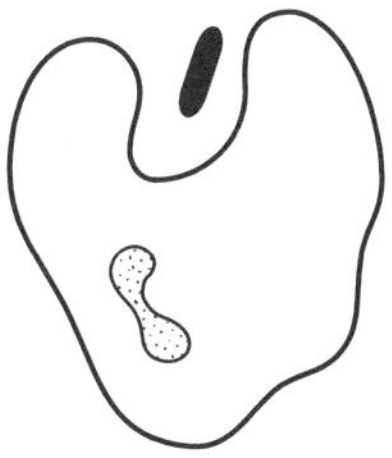

The correct order for these stages is

A 4 1 3 2

B 2 4 1 3

C 4 2 1 3

D 1 3 2 4.

**Questions 6 and 7** refer to the diagrams of cells below.

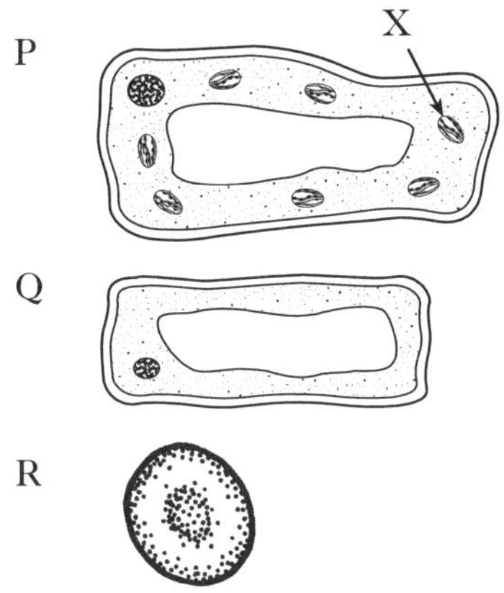


**6.** Which cells are plant cells?

A P only

B P and Q

C P and R

D R only

**7.** The function of structure X is to

A control all cell activities

B keep the cell turgid

C produce glucose using light energy

D release energy from glucose.

**8.** Lipase is an enzyme found in the small intestine. Lipase speeds up the breakdown of fat. Full cream milk contains a high proportion of fat.

Three test tubes were set up as shown in the diagrams below.

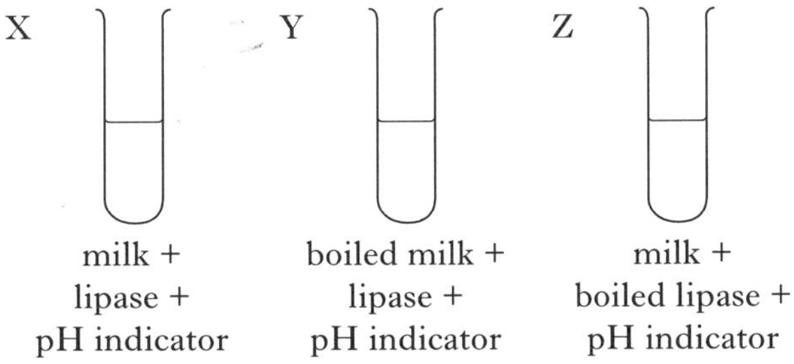


The pH of the contents of each test tube was recorded at the start and again 15 minutes later.

What changes in pH took place?

A The pH decreased in each test tube.

B The pH increased in each test tube.

C The pH decreased in tubes X and Y and did not change in tube Z.

D The pH increased in tubes Y and Z and did not change in tube X.

**Questions 9 and 10** refer to the bar chart below.

The bar chart shows the volume of blood supplied per minute to the skeletal muscles and to other parts of the body of a healthy male at rest and during strenuous exercise.

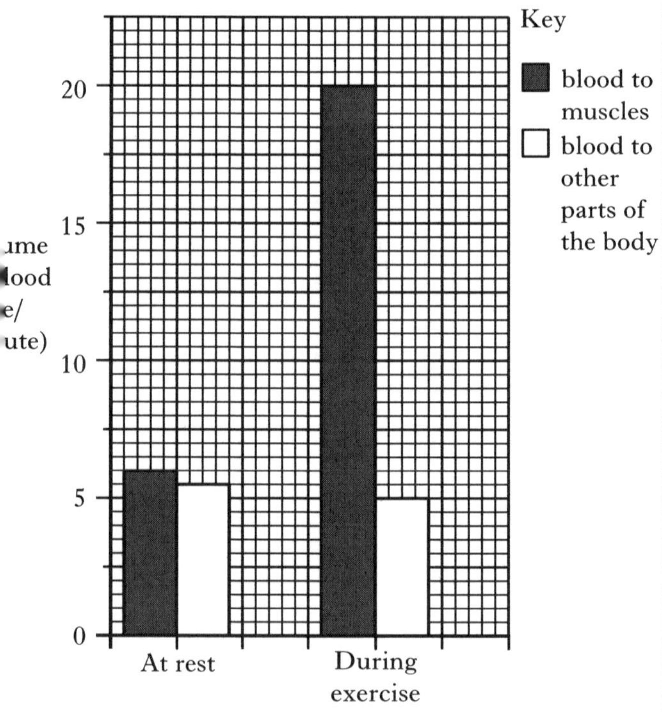


**9.** There is a difference in the volume of blood supplied per minute to the muscles and to other parts of the body **at rest**.

Which statement below is correct?

A 0·5 litre more blood is supplied to the muscles than to other parts of the body.

B 1·0 litre less blood is supplied to the muscles than to other parts of the body.

C 0·5 litre less blood is supplied to the muscles than to other parts of the body.

D 1·0 litre more blood is supplied to the muscles than to other parts of the body.

**10.** During **exercise**, the ratio of blood supplied to the muscles to blood supplied to other parts of the body is

A 1 : 4

B 4 : 1

C 6 : 5

D 10 : 3.

**11.** Haemoglobin combines with oxygen to form oxy-haemoglobin.

Which of the following statements is correct?

A At low oxygen levels oxy-haemoglobin releases oxygen in the lungs.

B At high oxygen levels oxy-haemoglobin releases oxygen in the tissues.

C At low oxygen levels oxy-haemoglobin releases oxygen in the tissues.

D At high oxygen levels oxy-haemoglobin releases oxygen in the lungs.

**Questions 12 and 13** refer to the diagram of the brain below.

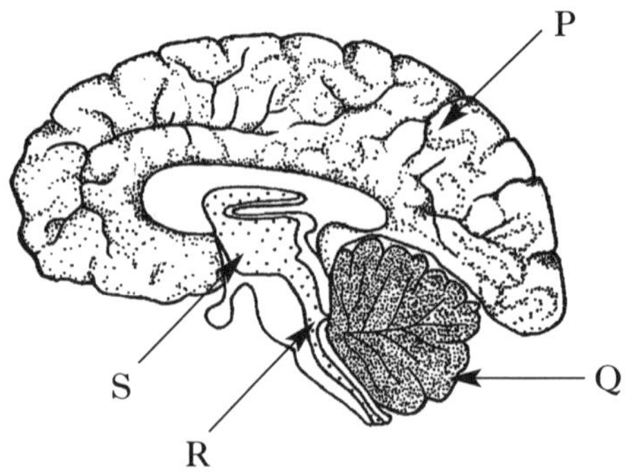


**12.** The part labelled **P** is the

A cerebrum

B cerebellum

C medulla

D hypothalamus.

**13.** The hypothalamus

A is responsible for conscious responses

B co-ordinates activities in all parts of the body

C detects changes in the water content of the blood

D controls the heart and breathing rates.

**[Turn over**

**14.** Dried yeast was mixed with flour and sugar solution to make dough.

The dough was put into a measuring cylinder as shown in the diagram below.

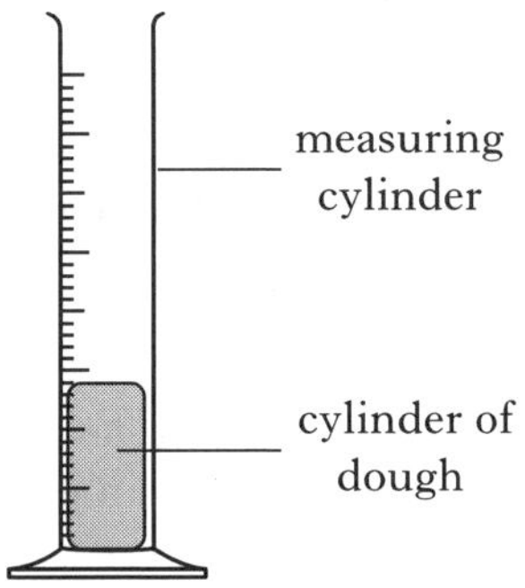


The volume of dough was measured over a 40 minute period.

The results are shown in the table below.

| *Time (minutes)* | 0 | 10 | 20 | 30 | 40 |
|---|---|---|---|---|---|
| *Volume of dough* ($cm^3$) | 25 | 27 | 31 | 37 | 40 |

The percentage increase in the volume of the dough from the start to the end of the period was

A 15

B 37·5

C 60

D 62·5.

**15.** Which of the following statements is correct?

A Anaerobic respiration produces 38 molecules of ATP from each glucose molecule.

B Anaerobic respiration produces twice as much energy as aerobic respiration.

C Aerobic respiration produces 38 molecules of ATP from each glucose molecule.

D Aerobic respiration produces 2 molecules of ATP from each glucose molecule.

**16.** Which of the following is a **reversible** reaction in anaerobic respiration?

A The conversion of pyruvic acid to ethanol and carbon dioxide

B The conversion of glucose to pyruvic acid

C The conversion of pyruvic acid to carbon dioxide and water

D The conversion of pyruvic acid to lactic acid

**17.** A piece of potato was cut from a potato tuber, blotted dry and weighed.

It was placed in pure water for an hour and then removed, dried and re-weighed.

It was then placed in concentrated sugar solution for an hour, removed, dried and re-weighed.

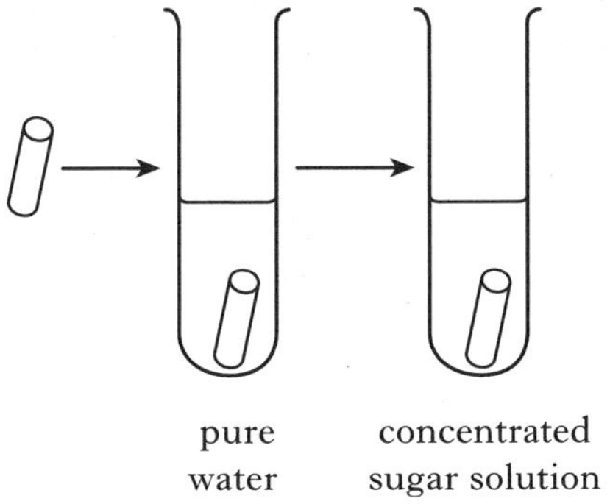


Which line in the table shows the results most likely to be obtained?

| | *First weight* (g) | *Second weight* (g) | *Third weight* (g) |
|---|---|---|---|
| A | 5 | 6 | 4 |
| B | 5 | 4 | 6 |
| C | 5 | 7 | 9 |
| D | 5 | 4 | 3 |

**Questions 18 and 19** refer to the diagram below.

The diagram represents energy flow in a woodland ecosystem.

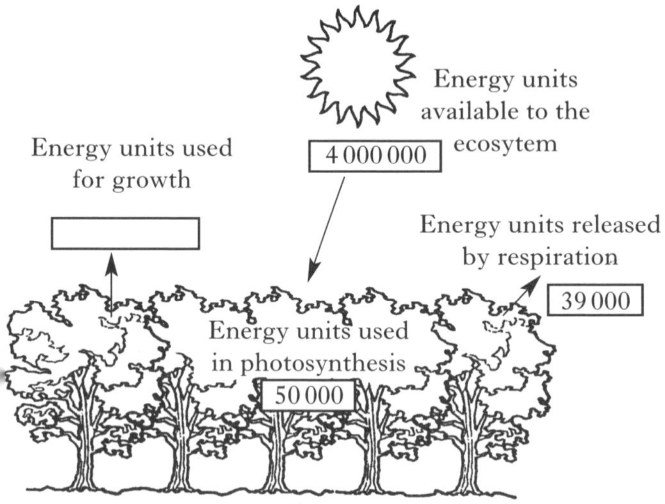


**18.** The number of energy units used for growth is

A 11 000

B 89 000

C 3 950 000

D 3 961 000.

**19.** The percentage of the energy from sunlight absorbed by trees and used for photosynthesis is

A 1·25

B 12·5

C 98·75

D 8000.

**20.** The diagram below shows the pyramid of energy for a food chain.

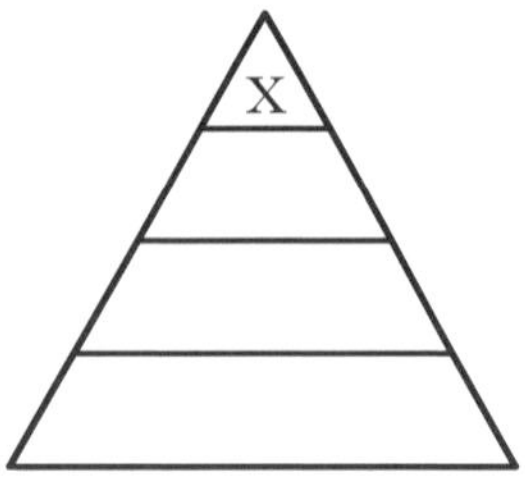


There is less energy at level X in the pyramid because

A energy is stored in each level and not passed on

B energy is lost at each level in a food chain

C the energy is concentrated in fewer organisms

D organisms in level X are very small.

**21.** The table below shows the relationship between planting density and the mass of seed harvested for a trial cereal crop.

| *Planting density (number of plants per square metre)* | *Mass of seed harvested (grammes per square metre)* |
|---|---|
| 4 | 60 |
| 8 | 86 |
| 16 | 104 |
| 32 | 77 |
| 128 | 22 |

The reason a low mass of seed was harvested when the planting density was 128 plants per square metre was

A less disease at high planting densities

B more nutrients available

C more competition for light and nutrients

D less space for weeds.

**[Turn over**

**Questions 22 and 23** refer to the graph below.

The graph shows the variations in the populations of arctic hares and their predators, foxes, in an area.

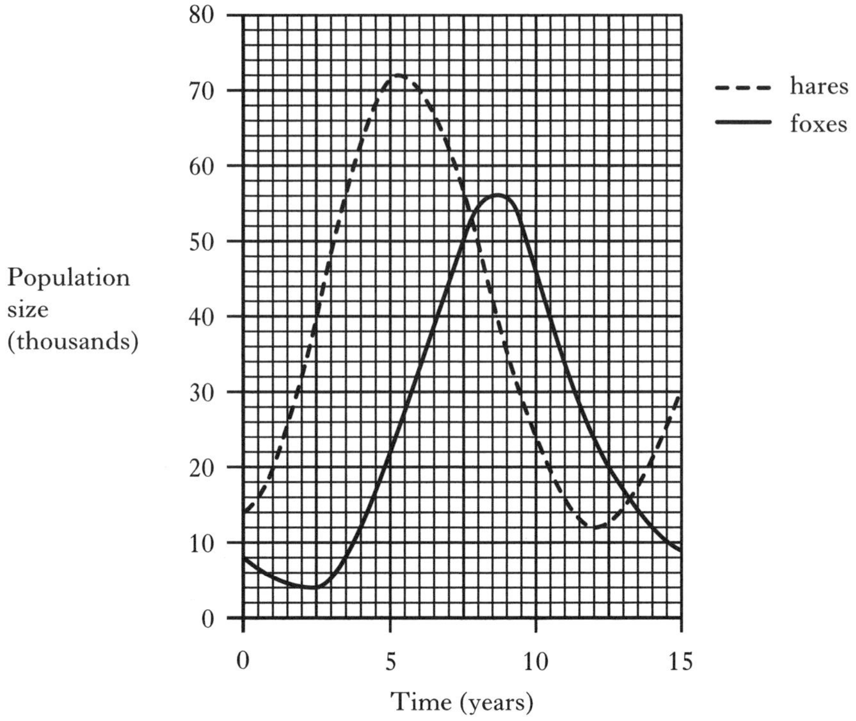


**22.** What is the difference in the population sizes of the hares and foxes when both populations are at their maximum?

A 3 000

B 16 000

C 52 000

D 58 000

**23.** What could be the reason for the decline in number of foxes after 9 years?

A The food available decreased.

B The numbers of prey increased.

C There is less disease in both populations.

D The food available increased.

**24.** The table below gives information about chromosomes in some human cells.

Which line in the table is correct?

| | *Cell* | *Number of chromosome sets* | *Number of chromosomes* |
|---|---|---|---|
| A | nerve | 2 | 23 |
| B | egg | 1 | 23 |
| C | lymphocyte | 1 | 46 |
| D | sperm | 2 | 23 |

**25.** When a plant with red flowers was crossed with a plant with white flowers, the $F_1$ plants had pink flowers.

The $F_1$ plants were then self-fertilised.

What ratio of flower colours would be found in the $F_2$ generation?

A 1 red : 2 white

B 1 white : 2 pink

C 1 red : 2 pink : 1 white

D 1 red : 1 pink : 1 white

**Candidates are reminded that the answer sheet for Section A MUST be placed <u>inside</u> the front cover of this answer book.**

DO NOT WRITE IN THIS MARGIN

## SECTION B

**All questions in this section should be attempted.**

*Marks*

**1.** (*a*) The diagram below shows a capillary network similar to that found surrounding air sacs in the lungs.

State **two** features of the **capillary network** in the lungs that allow efficient gas exchange to take place.

Explain how each feature improves gas exchange.

Feature 1 ____________________________ **1**

Explanation ____________________________ **1**

Feature 2 ____________________________ **1**

Explanation ____________________________ **1**

(*b*) The diagram below shows gas exchange taking place in the tissues.

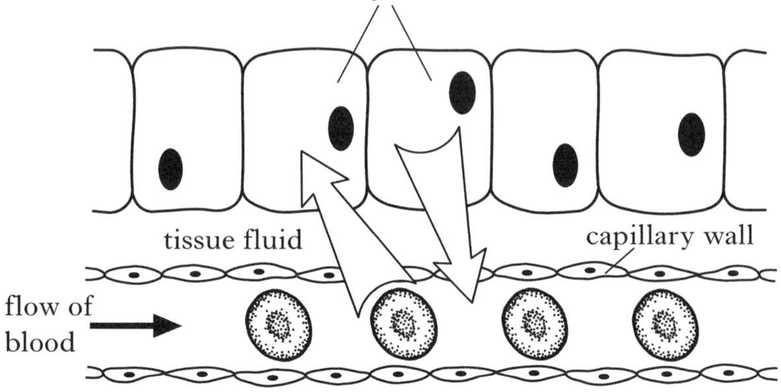


Name the process by which gases pass between capillaries and body cells.

____________________________ **1**

*Marks*

**2.** The bar graph below shows average blood pressure measurements in different blood vessels for a healthy individual.

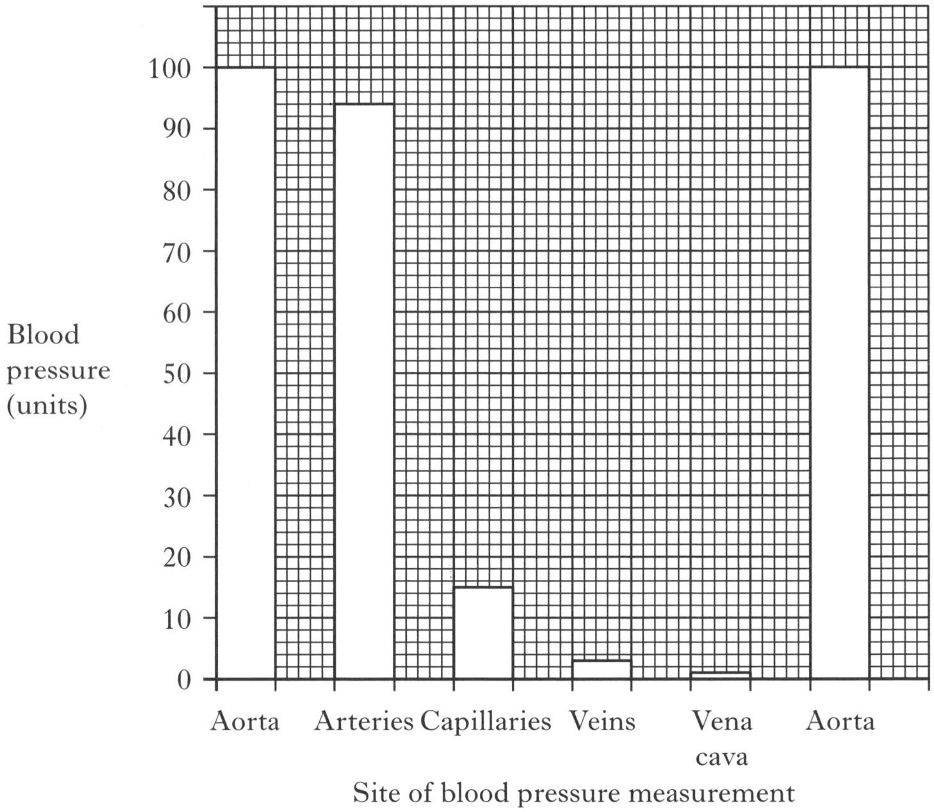


(*a*) Calculate the **simple whole number ratio** of the blood pressure in the aorta to the blood pressure found in the capillaries.

*Space for calculation*

__________ : __________ **1**

(*b*) Calculate the **percentage decrease** in blood pressure when blood moves from a capillary to a vein.

*Space for calculation*

__________ % **1**

(*c*) Explain what brings about the large increase in blood pressure between the vena cava and the aorta.

________________________________________ **1**

(*d*) The blood pressure in veins is very low.

Name the structures in veins that prevent blood flowing backwards.

________________________________________ **1**

DO NOT WRITE IN THIS MARGIN

*Marks*

**3.** An investigation was carried out into the concentration of lactic acid in the blood before, during and after a two minute period of strenuous exercise.

The results are shown in the graph below.

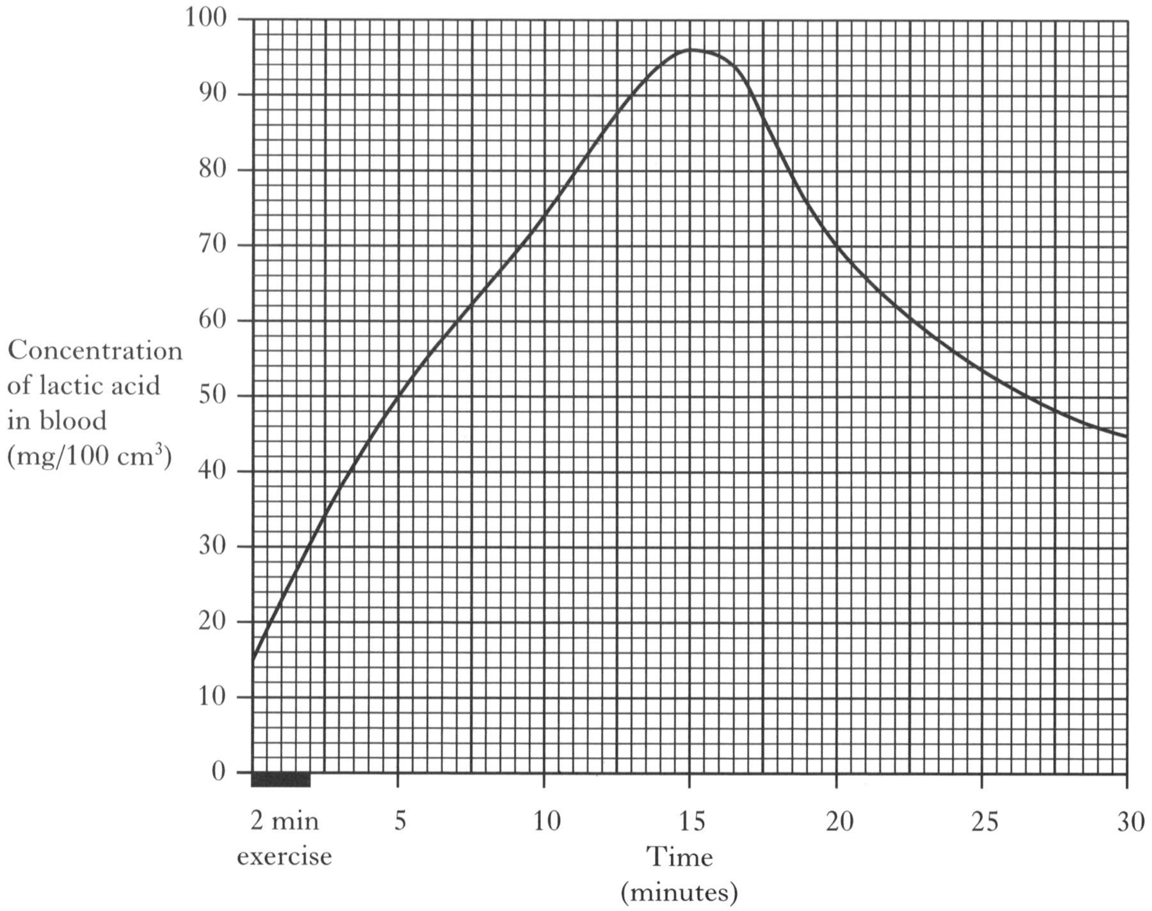


(*a*) What was the concentration of lactic acid in the blood ten minutes after the start of the exercise?

_______________ $mg/100\,cm^3$ **1**

(*b*) Explain why the concentration of lactic acid in the blood increased during and immediately after the strenuous exercise.

______________________________________________

______________________________________________ **1**

(*c*) What caused the lactic acid concentration to decrease 15 minutes after the start of the exercise?

______________________________________________

______________________________________________ **1**

DO NOT WRITE IN THIS MARGIN

*Marks*

**4.** (*a*) The table below shows the composition of four foods.

| *Food* | *Food Components* | | | | |
|---|---|---|---|---|---|
| | *Carbohydrate* % | *Fat* % | *Protein* % | *Water* % | *Other* % |
| Meat | 0 | 18 | 18 | 62 | 2 |
| Milk | 5 | 5 | 4 | 86 | 0 |
| Maize | 10 | 2 | 7 | 78 | 3 |
| Soya Beans | 34 | 18 | 34 | 9 | 5 |

(i) Complete the bar graph by

1. putting a scale on the vertical axis
2. adding the bar to show all the components of meat.

(Additional graph paper, if required, will be found on page 32.)

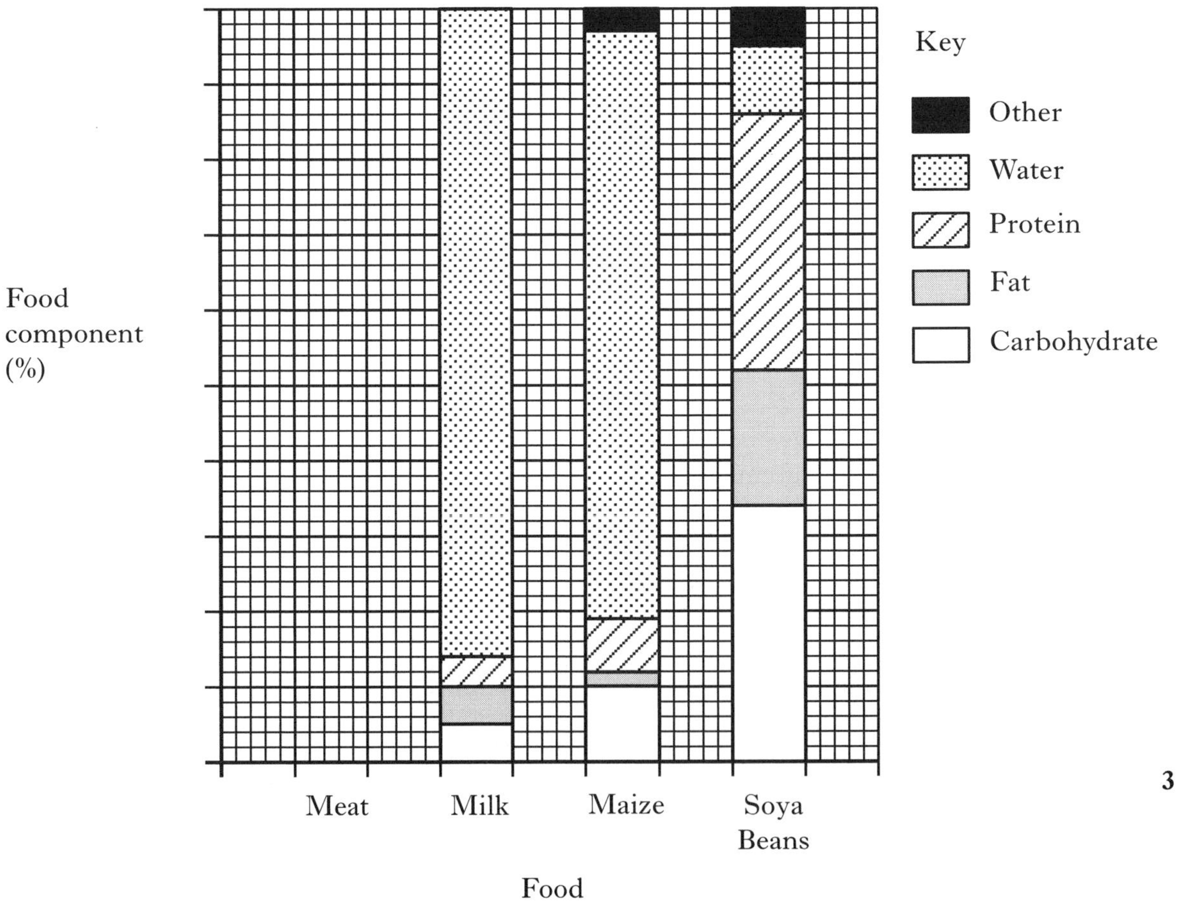


3

DO NOT WRITE IN THIS MARGIN

*Marks*

**4. (*a*) (continued)**

(ii) The final column in the table has been headed "other".

Name **one** of the food groups which is included under this heading.

________________________________ **1**

(iii) Which component of food is needed to produce enzymes?

________________________________ **1**

(*b*) Name the **three** elements common to carbohydrate, protein and fat.

____________________________________________________________ **1**

**[Turn over**

Marks

**5.** The diagram below shows some of the structures involved in a reflex action.

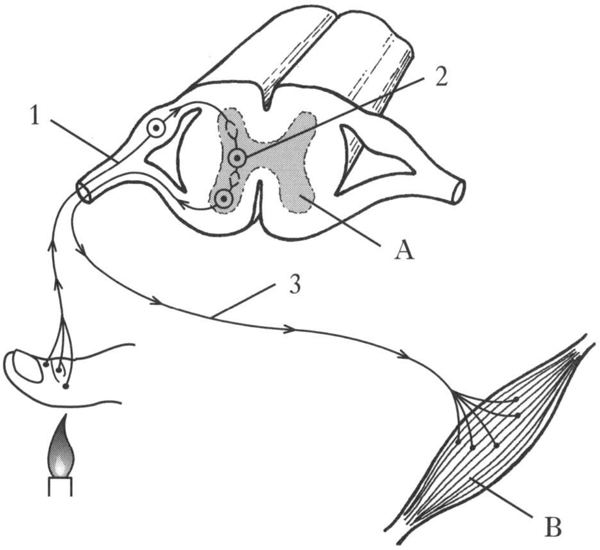


(*a*) The neurones labelled 1, 2 and 3 form a reflex arc.

Name each of these neurones.

1 ______________________

2 ______________________

3 ______________________ **2**

(*b*) Some neurones found in area A may transmit impulses to another part of the Central Nervous System (CNS).

Name the part of the CNS which receives these impulses.

______________________ **1**

(*c*) Describe the response that occurs at B.

______________________ **1**

(*d*) What is the function of reflex actions?

______________________ **1**

DO NOT WRITE IN THIS MARGIN

*Marks*

**6.** (*a*) A freshwater fish is hypertonic to its environment.

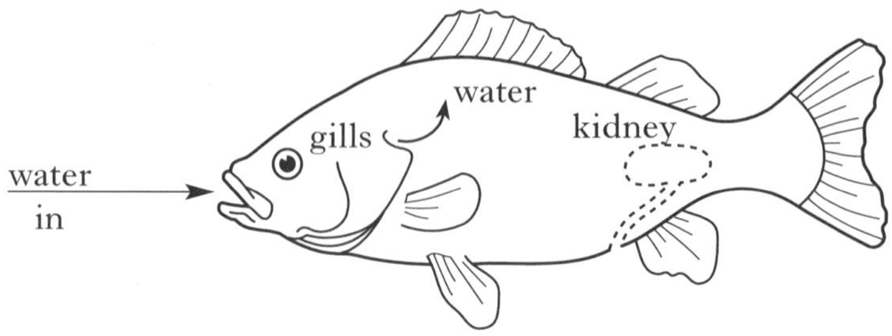


Underline **one** option in each set of brackets to make the sentences below correct.

The gills of this fish { take in / give out } salts.

The kidneys produce a { large / small } volume of { dilute / concentrated } urine. **2**

(*b*) (i) Name the hormone that acts on the kidney to maintain water balance in humans.

____________________________________ **1**

(ii) Name the part of the kidney nephron on which the hormone has its effect.

____________________________________ **1**

(iii) When the concentration of water in the blood increases, the hormone acts to return the water concentration to normal.

What term is used to describe this mechanism?

____________________________________ **1**

**[Turn over**

Marks

**7.** Albumin is a protein which can be broken down by the enzyme trypsin.

When albumin is added to agar the agar becomes cloudy.

When the albumin is broken down by trypsin the agar becomes clear.

$$\text{albumin} \xrightarrow{\text{trypsin}} \text{amino acids}$$

Groups of students carried out an investigation to find the effect of pH on the activity of the enzyme trypsin.

Each group carried out the following procedure.

1. A petri dish containing cloudy albumin agar was collected.
2. Three wells were cut out of the agar.
3. Drops of trypsin and buffer solution of different pH were added to the wells, as shown in the diagram below.

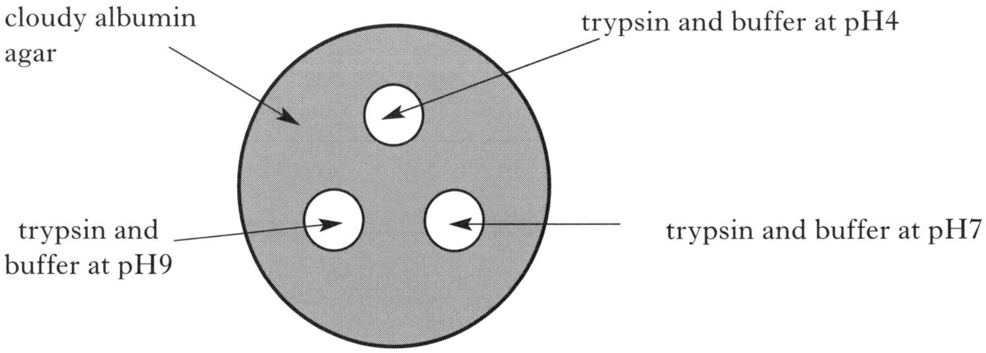


4. The dishes were incubated at 37 °C for 24 hours.
5. The diameter of the clear zone around each well was measured.

(*a*) State **one** variable that should have been kept constant when the dishes were set up.

______________________________________________ **1**

DO NOT WRITE IN THIS MARGIN

*Marks*

**7. (continued)**

(*b*) The results from each group are given in the table below.

| | *Diameter of the clear area* (mm) | | | | |
|---|---|---|---|---|---|
| *pH* | *Group 1* | *Group 2* | *Group 3* | *Group 4* | *Average* |
| 4 | 1 | 2 | 0 | 3 | 1·5 |
| 7 | 6 | 9 | 8 | 11 | |
| 9 | 21 | 23 | 20 | 24 | 22 |

(i) Complete the table by calculating the average diameter of the clear area for pH7. **1**

*Space for calculation*

(ii) Explain why the results for all groups were collected and averages calculated.

______________________________________________ **1**

(iii) From the results, describe the effect of pH on the activity of trypsin.

______________________________________________ **1**

(*c*) One group suggested setting up a control to show that the enzyme caused the observed effects.

Complete the labels on the diagram below to show the content of the wells for the control. **1**

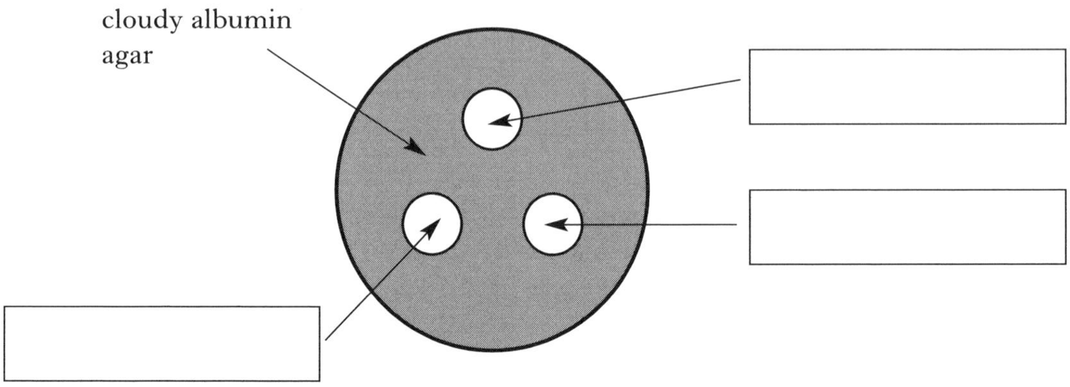


**[Turn over**

DO N
WRIT
TH
MAR

*Marks*

**8.** (*a*) A scientist grew some cereal plants in a field.

During the course of a day, she removed 2 plants every 4 hours and measured the concentrations of sugar in the leaves of the plants.

The results are shown in the table below.

| | *Sugar concentration (percentage of dry mass)* | | |
|---|---|---|---|
| *Time of day (hours)* | *Sample 1* | *Sample 2* | *Average* |
| 0400 | 0·42 | 0·48 | 0·45 |
| 0800 | 0·58 | 0·62 | 0·60 |
| 1200 | 1·46 | 2·04 | 1·75 |
| 1600 | 1·57 | 2·43 | 2·00 |
| 2000 | 1·05 | 1·75 | 1·40 |
| 2400 | 0·49 | 0·51 | 0·50 |

Present the results in an appropriate format on the grid below.
(Additional graph paper, if required, will be found on page 33.)

3

DO NOT WRITE IN THIS MARGIN

*Marks*

**8. (continued)**

(*b*) The following word equation shows the first stage of photosynthesis.

$$\text{water} \xrightarrow{\text{light energy}} \text{oxygen + hydrogen + ATP}$$

(i) Name this stage of photosynthesis.

________________________ **1**

(ii) Describe what happens to each of the products.

Oxygen ________________________________

________________________________ **1**

Hydrogen ________________________________

________________________________ **1**

ATP ________________________________

________________________________ **1**

**[Turn over**

DO NOT WRITE IN THIS MARGIN

*Marks*

**9.** (*a*) Lettuces may be grown in "tunnels" covered in clear polythene as shown in the diagram below.

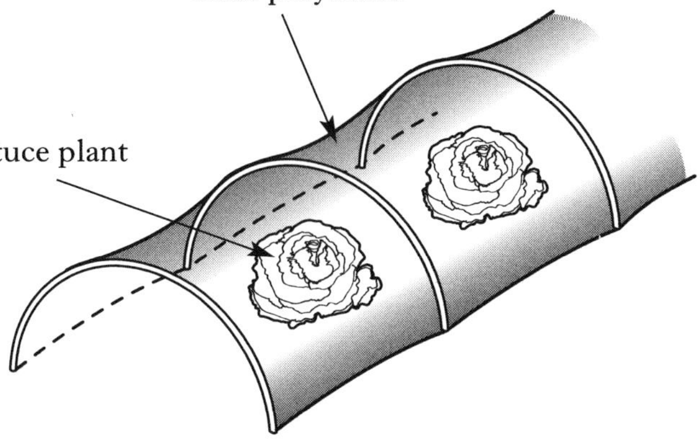


(i) Give **two** reasons why the use of clear polythene may result in the lettuces being ready for cropping earlier.

1 ______________________________

2 ______________________________ **2**

(ii) Air rich in carbon dioxide can be passed through these tunnels.

Explain how this would make the lettuces grow faster.

______________________________ **1**

DO NOT WRITE IN THIS MARGIN

*Marks*

**9. (continued)**

(*b*) The graph below shows how the rate of photosynthesis is affected by light intensity at different concentrations of carbon dioxide.

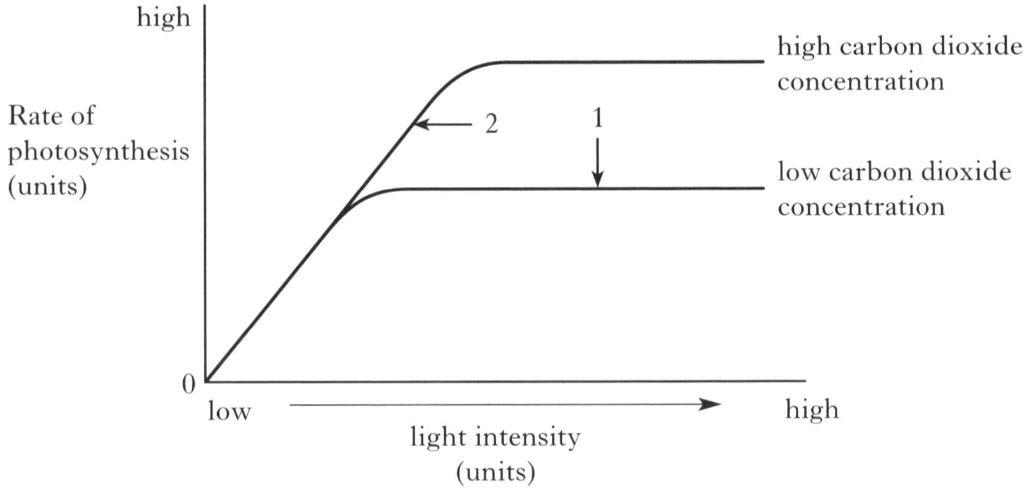


(i) What factor was limiting the rate of photosynthesis at points 1 and 2?

Point 1 ______________________________ **1**

Point 2 ______________________________ **1**

(ii) Name **one** other factor that may limit the rate of photosynthesis.

______________________________ **1**

**[Turn over**

DO NOT WRITE IN THIS MARGIN

*Marks*

**10.** (*a*) In peas the height of the plant is controlled by one gene which has two alleles.

T represents the dominant allele for tall stems.

t represents the allele for short stems.

True breeding, tall-stemmed pea plants were crossed with short-stemmed pea plants to produce the $F_1$ generation.

(i) State the genotype of the parents.

__________ and __________ **1**

(ii) State the phenotypes of the $F_1$ plants.

________________________________________ **1**

(iii) Plants from the $F_1$ generation were crossed to produce the $F_2$ generation of plants.

State the phenotypes and their expected ratio in the $F_2$ generation.

________________ : ________________ plants **1**

DO NOT WRITE IN THIS MARGIN

*Marks*

**10. (continued)**

(*b*) Seeds from true breeding, tall-stemmed pea plants were provided with different growing conditions as shown in the diagrams below.

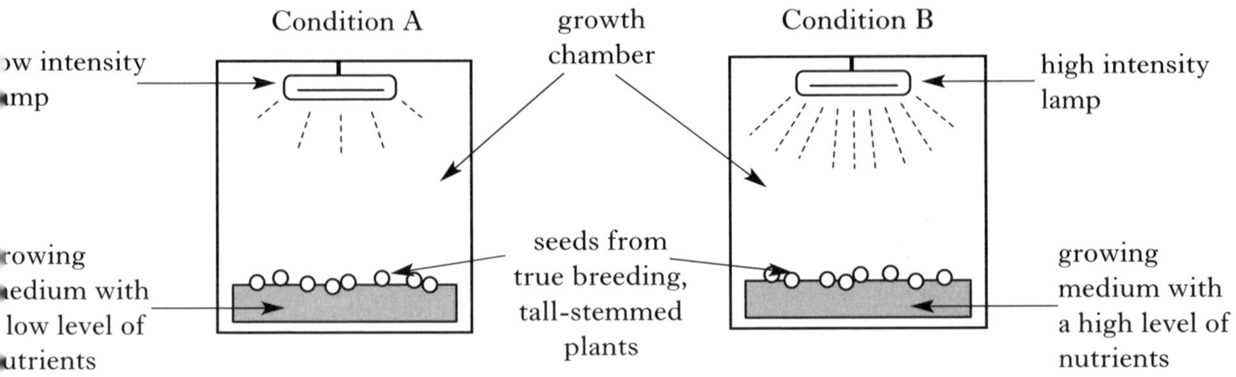


(i) **Compare** the expected appearance of the plants in each group.

________________________________________

________________________________________ **1**

(ii) What term is used to describe the effect of different conditions on the phenotype of an organism?

________________________________________ **1**

**[Turn over**

DO NOT WRITE IN THIS MARGIN

*Marks*

**11.** The song thrush feeds on snails which it finds by sight in a variety of habitats.

Snails are herbivores and feed only on grasses.

(*a*) (i) Present this feeding relationship as a food chain. **1**

(ii) Use the information above to complete the table below.

| *Term* | *Organism* |
|---|---|
| primary consumer | snail |
| predator | |
| prey | |
| producer | |

**2**

(iii) Describe what is meant by a *habitat*.

______________________________ **1**

(*b*) Name a decomposer and describe the role of decomposers in an ecosystem.

Decomposer ______________________________ **1**

Role of decomposers ______________________________ **1**

DO NOT WRITE IN THIS MARGIN

Marks

**11. (continued)**

(*c*) The snail *Cepea* shows variation in shell colour and different forms of shell are found.

Two of the forms are shown below.

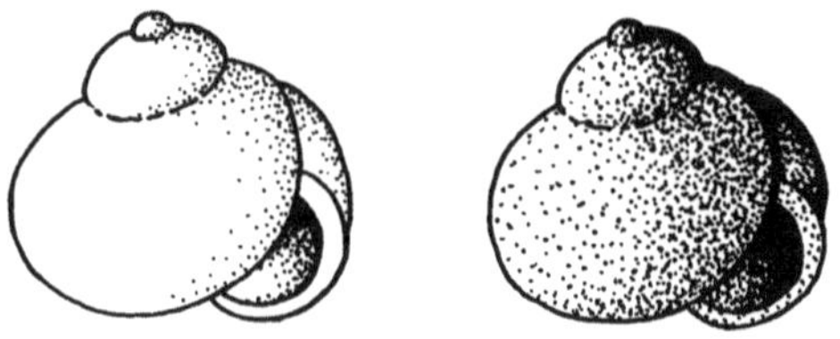

Light form    Dark form

The table below shows the results of an investigation into the numbers of different forms of snails found in two habitats.

| *Habitat* | *Light form* | *Dark form* | *Other forms* |
|---|---|---|---|
| dense woodland | 14 | 64 | 22 |
| open grassland | 58 | 12 | 30 |

Explain how natural selection has resulted in the high numbers of the dark form of the shell in the **dense woodland**.

______________________________________________

______________________________________________

______________________________________________ 2

**[Turn over**

Marks

**12.** An investigation into the behaviour of blowfly larvae was carried out.

One blowfly larva was placed at X and then lamp A was switched on.

When the larva reached Y, lamp A was switched off and lamp B was switched on.

The path taken by the larva is shown in the diagram below.

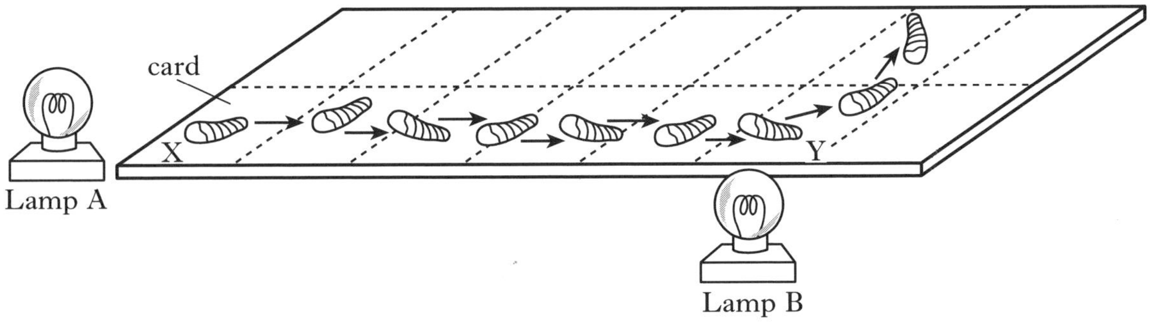


(*a*) Describe the response of the larva to light.

______________________________ **1**

(*b*) (i) Suggest **one** change to the apparatus that would confirm that the response was due to the light and not the heat from the lamp.

______________________________ **1**

(ii) State **one** way in which the reliability of the result could be improved.

______________________________ **1**

(*c*) (i) Name a stimulus, other than light, to which woodlice respond.

______________ **1**

(ii) Describe the response of woodlice to this stimulus.

______________________________ **1**

(iii) Explain the adaptive significance of this response in woodlice.

______________________________ **1**

**[Turn over for SECTION C on *Page twenty-eight***

DO N WRIT TH MAR

## SECTION C

**Both questions in this section should be attempted.**

Note that each question contains a choice.

**Questions 1 and 2 should be attempted on the blank pages which follow.**

**Supplementary sheets, if required, may be obtained from the invigilator.**

*Marks*

**In question 1, ONE mark is available for coherence.**

**1.** Answer **either** A **or** B.

A. The maps below show the changes in distribution of the red squirrel in the UK from 1920 to 1990.

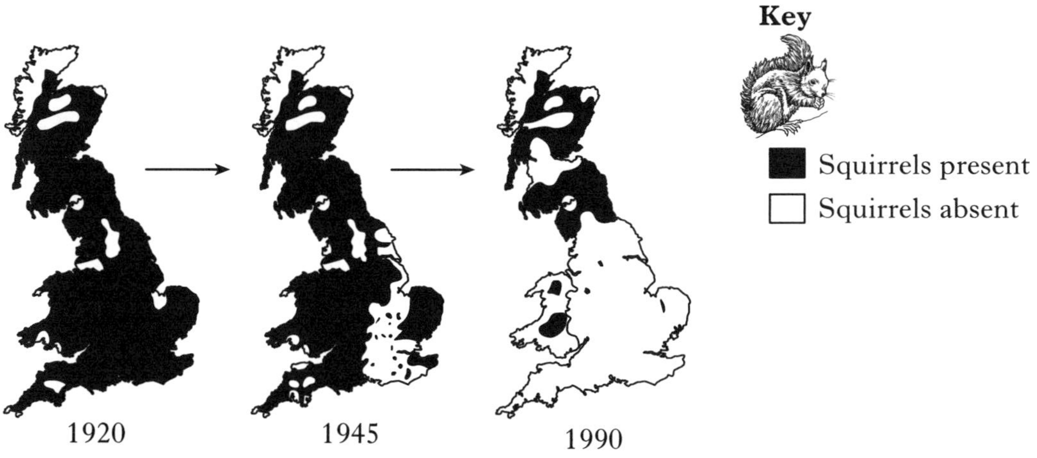


(*a*) Describe the change in distribution between 1920 and 1990.

(*b*) Suggest reasons for this change.

(*c*) Discuss the potential impact this could have on biodiversity. **5**

**OR**

B. The diagram below shows the two stages that result in the formation of offspring in animals.

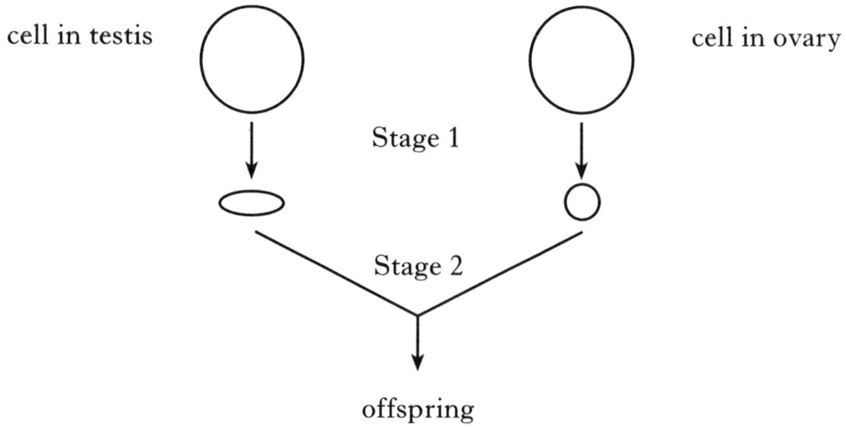


(*a*) Describe what happens at **each** stage.

(*b*) Explain how variation is brought about during **each** stage. **5**

**Question 2 is on *Page thirty*.**

DO NOT WRITE IN THIS MARGIN

*Marks*

**SPACE FOR ANSWER TO QUESTION 1**

DO NOT WRITE IN THIS MARGIN

*Marks*

**2.** Answer **either** A **or** B.

**Labelled diagrams may be included where appropriate.**

A. Give an account of the properties of enzymes. **5**

**OR**

B. Describe the stages in aerobic respiration. **5**

[*END OF QUESTION PAPER*]

DO NOT WRITE IN THIS MARGIN

**SPACE FOR ANSWER TO QUESTION 2**

**SPACE FOR ANSWERS**

ADDITIONAL GRAPH PAPER FOR QUESTION 4(*a*)(i)

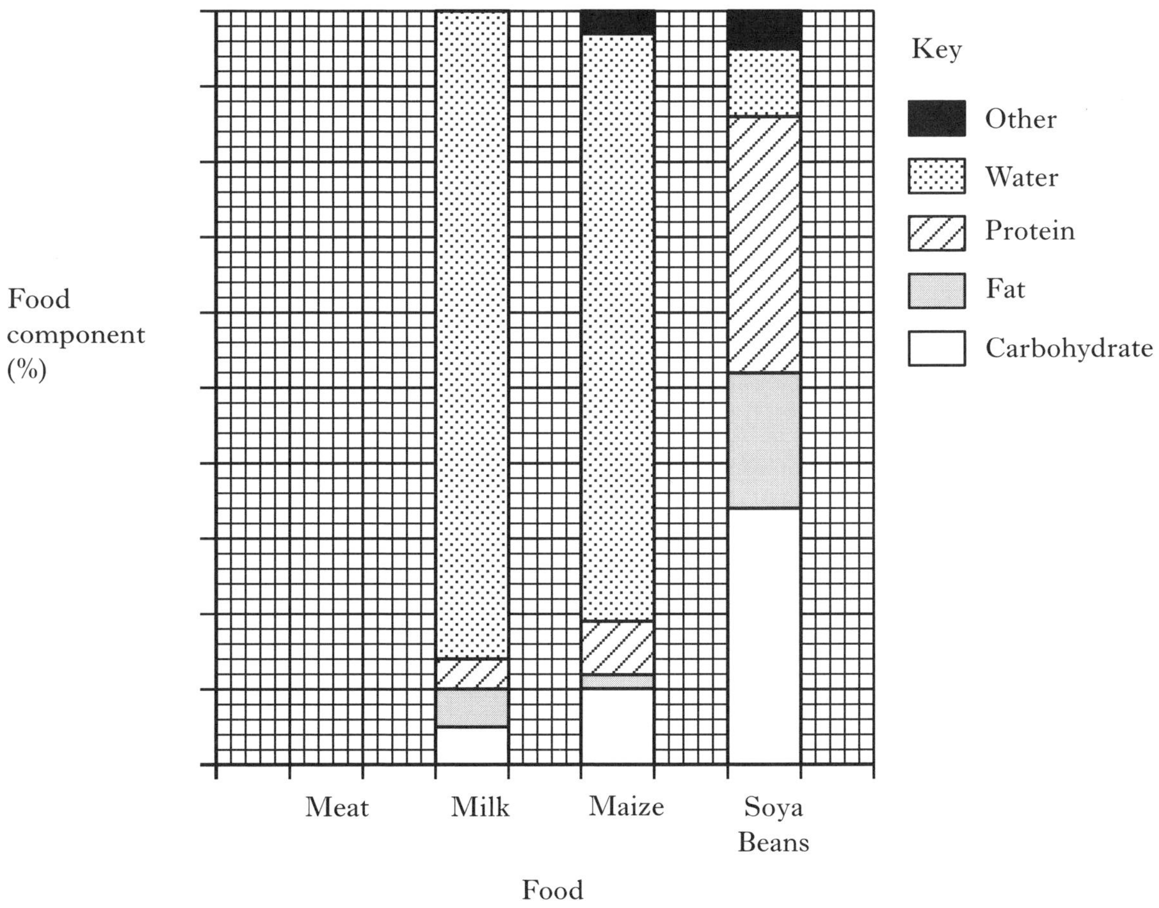

DO NOT WRITE IN THIS MARGIN

**SPACE FOR ANSWERS**

ADDITIONAL GRAPH PAPER FOR QUESTION 8(*a*)

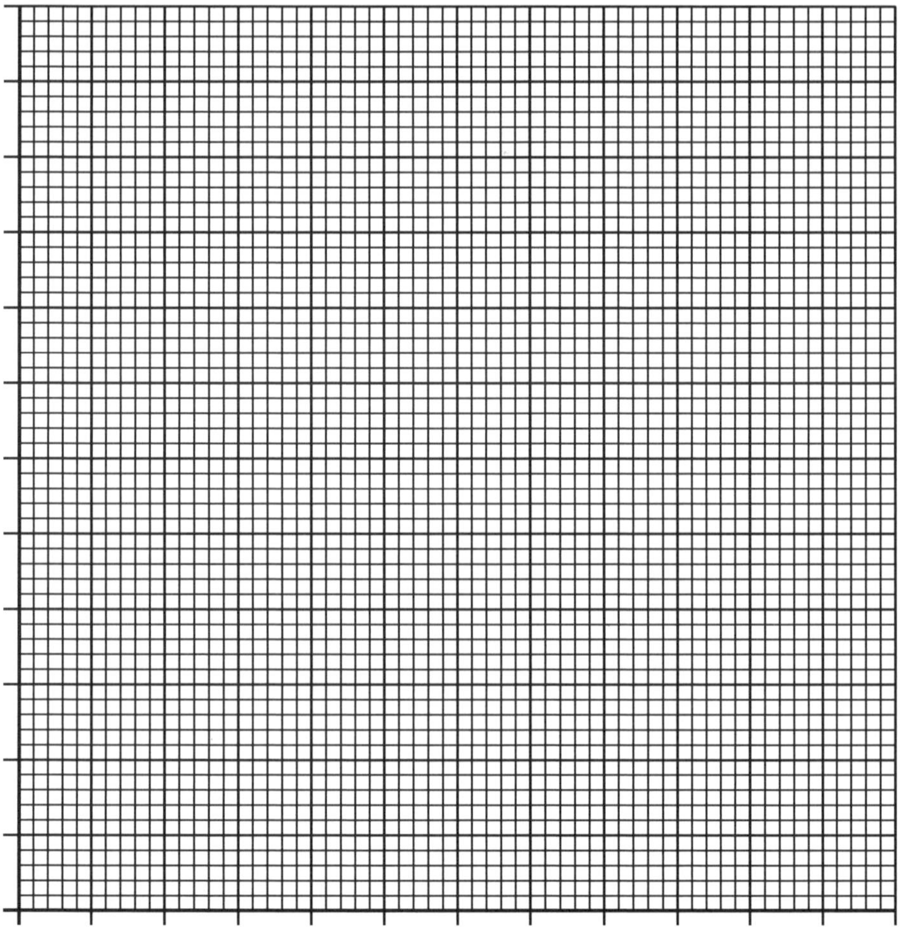

DO N
WRIT
TH
MAR

**SPACE FOR ANSWERS**

# INTERMEDIATE 2 2003

FOR OFFICIAL USE

| | | | | | |
|---|---|---|---|---|---|
| | | | | | |

Total for Sections B and C

# X007/201

NATIONAL QUALIFICATIONS 2003

MONDAY, 26 MAY
9.00 AM – 11.00 AM

# BIOLOGY
## INTERMEDIATE 2

**Fill in these boxes and read what is printed below.**

Full name of centre

Town

Forename(s)

Surname

Date of birth
Day Month Year

Scottish candidate number

Number of seat

**SECTION A (25 marks)**

Instructions for completion of Section A are given on page two.

**SECTIONS B AND C (75 marks)**

1 (a) All questions should be attempted.

(b) It should be noted that in **Section C** questions 1 and 2 each contain a choice.

2 The questions may be answered in any order but all answers are to be written in the spaces provided in this answer book, and must be written clearly and legibly in ink.

3 Additional space for answers and rough work will be found at the end of the book. If further space is required, supplementary sheets may be obtained from the invigilator and should be inserted inside the **front** cover of this book.

4 The numbers of questions must be clearly inserted with any answers written in the additional space.

5 Rough work, if any should be necessary, should be written in this book and then scored through when the fair copy has been written.

6 Before leaving the examination room you must give this book to the invigilator. If you do not, you may lose all the marks for this paper.

SCOTTISH QUALIFICATIONS AUTHORITY

**Read carefully**

1 Check that the answer sheet provided is for Biology Intermediate 2 (Section A).

2 Fill in the details required on the answer sheet.

3 In this section a question is answered by indicating the choice A, B, C or D by a stroke made in **ink** in the appropriate place in the answer sheet—see the sample question below.

4 For each question there is only **one** correct answer.

5 Rough working, if required, should be done only on this question paper, or on the rough working sheet provided—**not** on the answer sheet.

6 At the end of the examination the answer sheet for Section A **must** be placed inside the front cover of this answer book.

**Sample Question**

What must be present in leaf cells for photosynthesis to take place?

A Oxygen and water

B Carbon dioxide and water

C Carbon dioxide and oxygen

D Oxygen and hydrogen

**The correct answer is B**—Carbon dioxide and water. A **heavy** vertical line should be drawn joining the two dots in the appropriate box in the column headed **B** as shown **in the example on the answer sheet**.

If, after you have recorded your answer, you decide that you have made an error and wish to make a change, you should cancel the original answer and put a vertical stroke in the box you now consider to be correct. Thus, if you want to change an answer **D** to an answer **B**, your answer sheet would look like this:

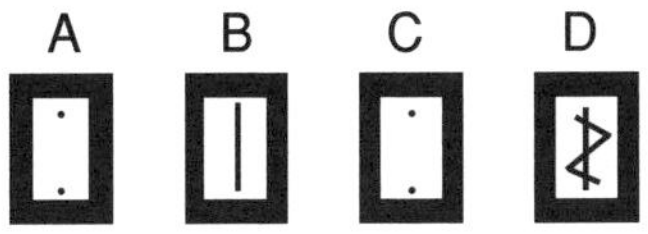


If you want to change back to an answer which has already been scored out, you should **enter a tick (✓)** to the RIGHT of the box of your choice, thus:

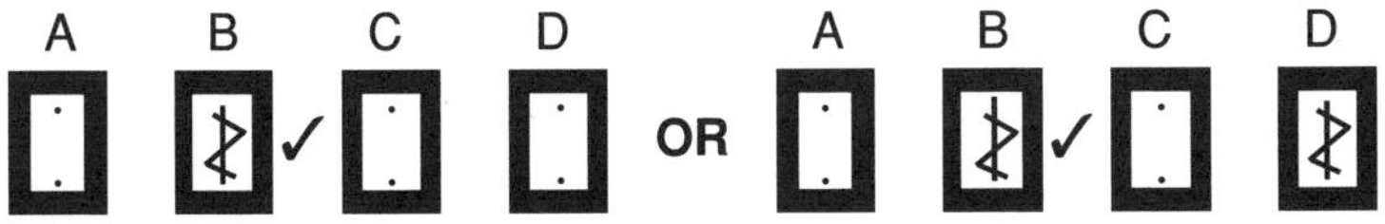

## SECTION A

**All questions in this Section should be attempted.**

**1.** Which carbohydrate is a component of cell walls?

A Glycogen

B Starch

C Cellulose

D Glucose

**2.** Enzymes act as catalysts because they

A are composed of protein

B act on all substrates

C raise energy input

D lower energy input.

**3.** The active site of an enzyme is complementary to

A one type of substrate molecule

B all types of substrate molecules

C one type of product molecule

D all types of product molecules.

**4.** Four thin sections of onion tissue were immersed in 5% sugar solution. The sections were left for 15 minutes then viewed under the microscope. The table shows the percentage of cells plasmolysed in each section.

| *Section* | *Cells plasmolysed* (%) |
|---|---|
| 1 | 22 |
| 2 | 22 |
| 3 | 27 |
| 4 | 29 |

The average percentage of cells plasmolysed is

A 22

B 25

C 27

D 100.

**5.** The breakdown of ATP in cells

A releases energy and produces ADP only

B releases energy and produces ADP + $P_i$

C requires energy and produces ADP only

D requires energy and produces ADP + $P_i$.

**6.** How many more ATP molecules are produced per glucose molecule by aerobic respiration than by anaerobic respiration?

A 2

B 19

C 36

D 38

**7.** Which of the following conditions in a greenhouse would produce earlier crops?

A Glass shading

B Cool air conditioners

C Additional oxygen

D Additional carbon dioxide

**8.** The diagram below shows a virus attached to a blood cell. The blood cell has responded by producing specific protein molecules labelled X.

(Diagram not drawn to scale.)

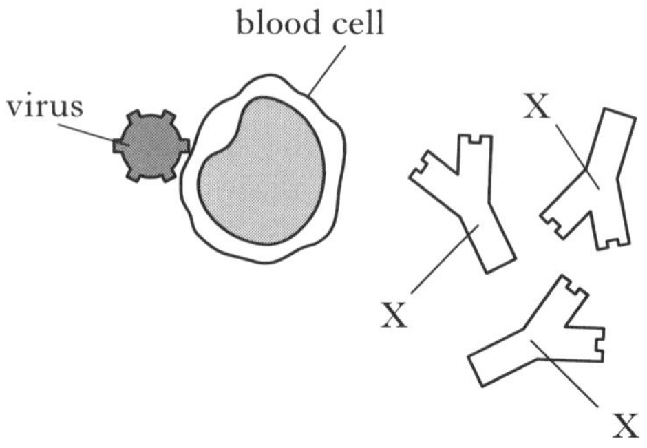


The molecules labelled X are

A antibodies

B antigens

C lymphocytes

D macrophages.

**9.** The table below refers to information about a breakfast cereal.

| *Ingredients* | *Mass per serving* |
|---|---|
| Protein | 6 g |
| Carbohydrate | 62 g |
| Fat | 4 g |
| Vitamins | 1·4 mg |
| Iron | 2·4 mg |

One serving will provide 20% of a child's daily requirement for iron.

How many mg of iron are required daily by a child?

A 0·12

B 0·48

C 12

D 48

**10.** The diagram below shows the movement of food along the oesophagus.

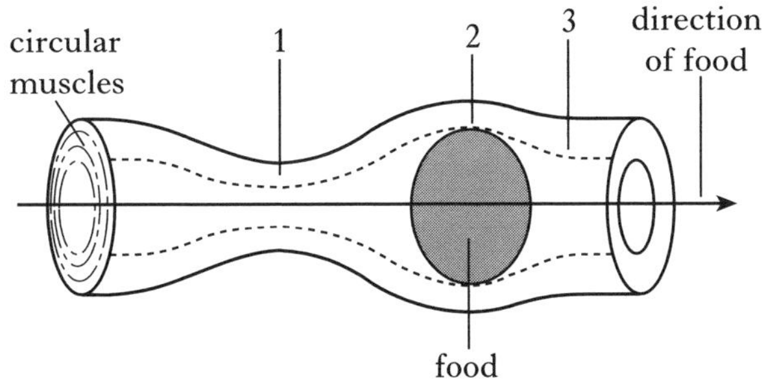


Which line in the table below correctly describes the state of the circular muscles at points 1, 2 and 3 on the diagram?

| | *Circular muscles* | | |
|---|---|---|---|
| | *Point 1* | *Point 2* | *Point 3* |
| A | contracted | relaxed | contracted |
| B | relaxed | contracted | contracted |
| C | contracted | relaxed | relaxed |
| D | relaxed | contracted | relaxed |

**11.** The following graph shows the results of an investigation into the effect of pH on the activity of four enzymes.

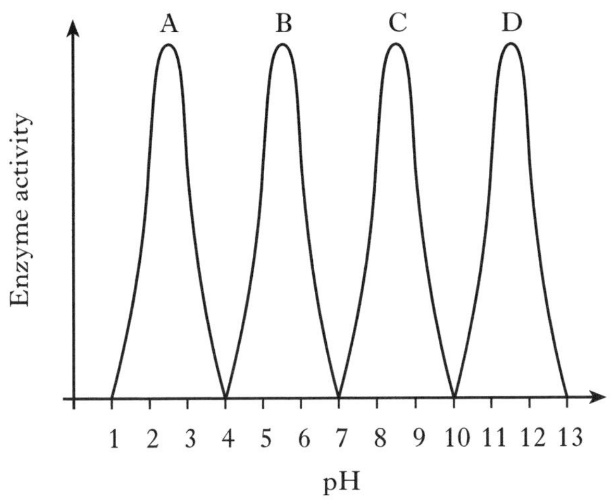


Which one of these enzymes could be pepsin in the stomach?

**12.** Which label correctly identifies the lacteal in the following diagram of a villus?

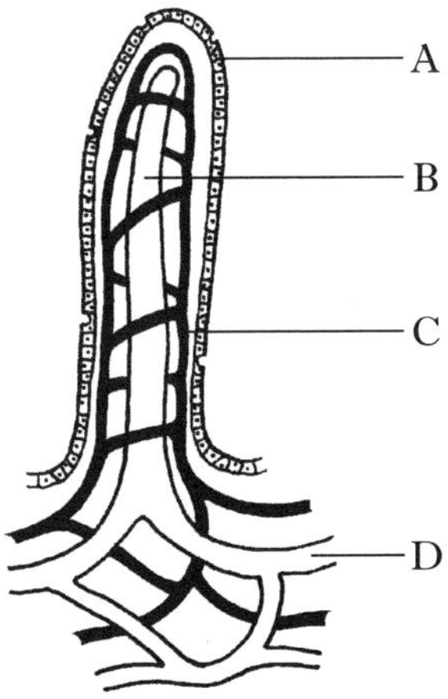


**13.** Which line in the table below correctly describes what happens to excess proteins in the diet?

| | *Site of deamination* | *Product* |
|---|---|---|
| A | liver | urea |
| B | kidney | urea |
| C | liver | amino acids |
| D | kidney | amino acids |

**14.** A food contains the elements carbon, hydrogen, oxygen and nitrogen. To which food group does it belong?

A Carbohydrates

B Proteins

C Fats

D Minerals

**Questions 15 and 16** refer to the table below which shows the composition of the blood entering the kidney and the composition of the urine leaving the kidney.

| *Substances* | *Composition of blood entering the kidney* (%) | *Composition of urine leaving the kidney* (%) |
|---|---|---|
| Water | 92 | 95 |
| Protein | 7 | 0 |
| Glucose | 0·10 | 0 |
| Salts | 0·37 | 0·60 |
| Urea | 0·03 | 2·00 |

**15.** Which of the following substances are all excreted by the kidney?

A Water, glucose and salts

B Water, salts and urea

C Salts, protein and urea

D Salts, glucose and protein

**16.** How many times greater is the urea concentration in urine than in blood?

A 0·015

B 0·06

C 1·97

D 66·67

**Questions 17 and 18** refer to the graph below which shows changes in blood pressure in the aorta during one heart beat cycle.

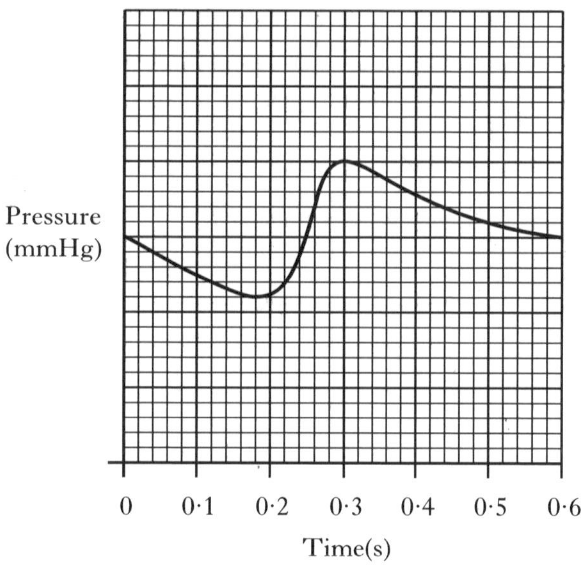


**17.** What is the heart rate in beats per minute?

A 30

B 60

C 100

D 120

**18.** At what time do the ventricles start to contract?

A 0·1s

B 0·2s

C 0·3s

D 0·4s

**[Turn over**

**19.** The diagram below shows a human sperm, egg and female zygote.

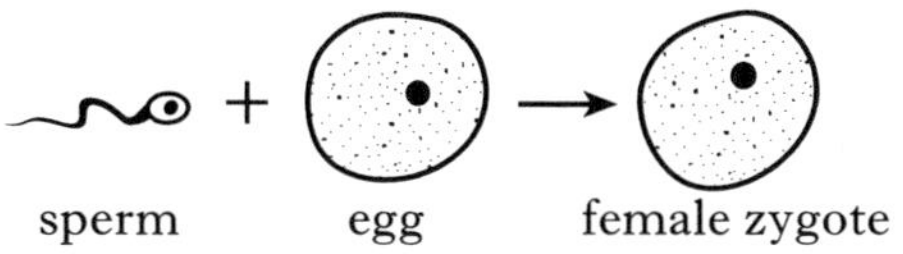


Which line in the table correctly describes the sex chromosomes in each of these cells?

| | *Sex chromosome(s) of sperm* | *Sex chromosome(s) of egg* | *Sex chromosome(s) of female zygote* |
|---|---|---|---|
| A | Y | X | XY |
| B | XY | XX | Y |
| C | XX | XY | X |
| D | X | X | XX |

**20.** A species can be defined as a group of organisms which

A contain identical genetic material

B have the same phenotypes

C contain the same number of chromosomes

D breed together to produce fertile offspring.

**Questions 21 and 22** refer to the following statements about a woodland ecosystem.

A All the oak trees

B All the plants

C All the plants and animals

D All the oak trees and blackbirds

**21.** Which statement describes a population?

**22.** Which statement describes a community?

**23.** A sample of fresh soil from a woodland ecosystem was weighed, dried in an oven at 95 °C for one week and reweighed.
The results are shown below.

Mass of fresh soil = 50 g
Mass of dried soil = 32 g

What percentage of the soil sample was water?

A 9

B 18

C 36

D 64

**24.** Which one of the following graphs shows the effects of competition for the same food between a successful species and an unsuccessful species?

Graph A

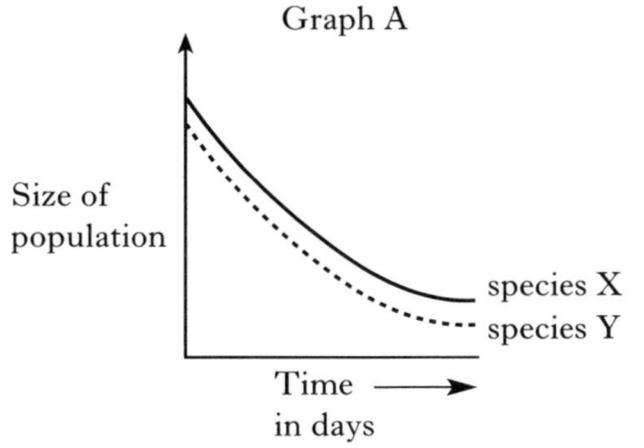


Graph B

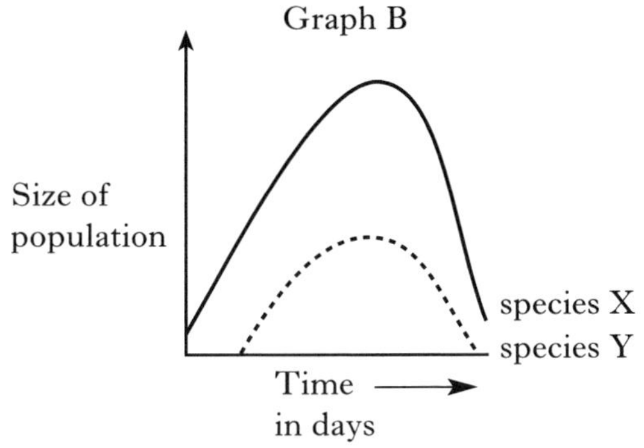


Graph C

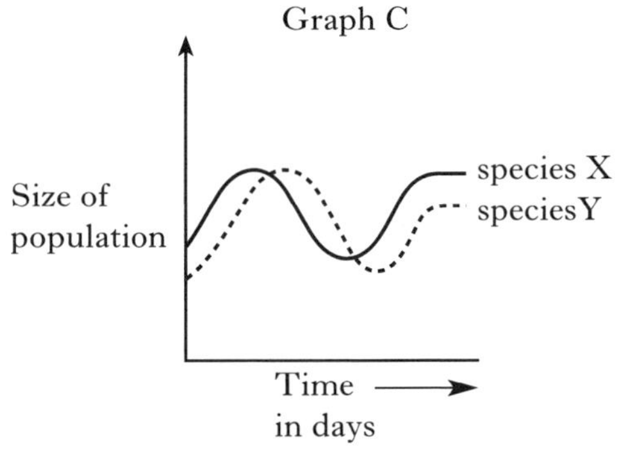


Graph D

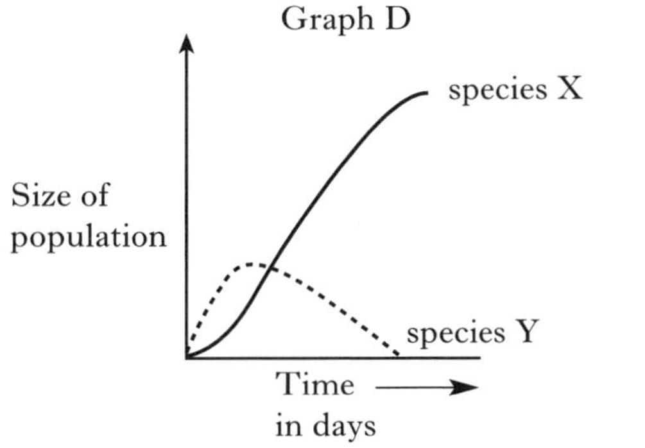

**25.** A river was sampled at six points along its length. The numbers of different animals, the oxygen concentration and the pH were recorded for each sampling point.

The results are shown in the table below.

| | *Sampling points* | | | | | |
|---|---|---|---|---|---|---|
| | 1 | 2 | 3 | 4 | 5 | 6 |
| Mayfly nymphs | 0 | 0 | 0 | 5 | 6 | 132 |
| Dragonfly nymphs | 1 | 1 | 0 | 0 | 1 | 1 |
| Chironimid fly larvae | 0 | 1 | 1 | 2 | 231 | 36 |
| Molluscs | 0 | 0 | 0 | 0 | 46 | 73 |
| Oxygen concentration (%) | 88 | 80 | 75 | 71 | 30 | 63 |
| pH | 5·6 | 6·0 | 6·5 | 7·3 | 7·5 | 8·0 |

Using these results identify which of the following conclusions is **correct**.

A Chironimid fly larvae do not survive in water of a low oxygen concentration.

B Molluscs survive better in water of a lower pH.

C The distribution of Dragonfly nymphs is not affected by changes in the pH and oxygen concentration of the water.

D The distribution of Mayfly nymphs is not affected by the oxygen concentration of the water.

**Candidates are reminded that the answer sheet for Section A MUST be placed <u>inside</u> the front cover of this answer book.**

**[Turn over for Section B on *Page nine***

**[BLANK PAGE]**

DO NOT WRITE IN THIS MARGIN

## SECTION B

**All questions in this section should be attempted.**

*Marks*

**1.** The diagram below shows a section through a plant cell.

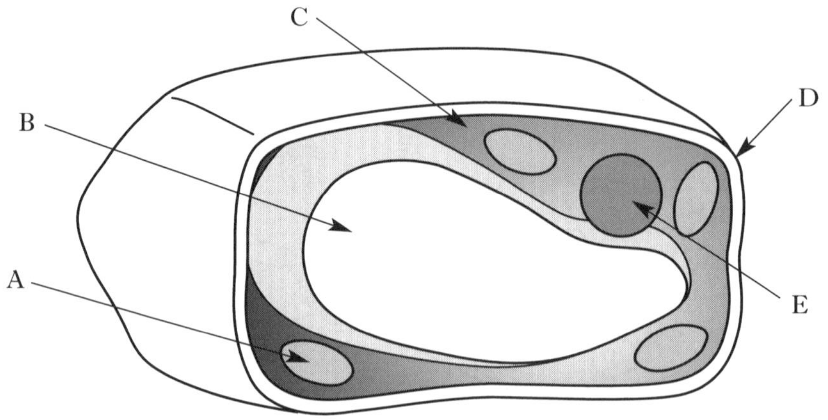


(*a*) (i) Which **two** letters identify structures found in both plant and animal cells?

__________

__________ **1**

(ii) Name the enzyme-controlled process associated with structure A.

________________________________________ **1**

(*b*) Name a molecule found in structure E which is composed of a sequence of bases.

________________________________________ **1**

**[Turn over**

DO NOT WRITE IN THIS MARGIN

*Marks*

**2.** The diagram below represents a section of human tissue showing an exchange of materials between the body cells and blood.

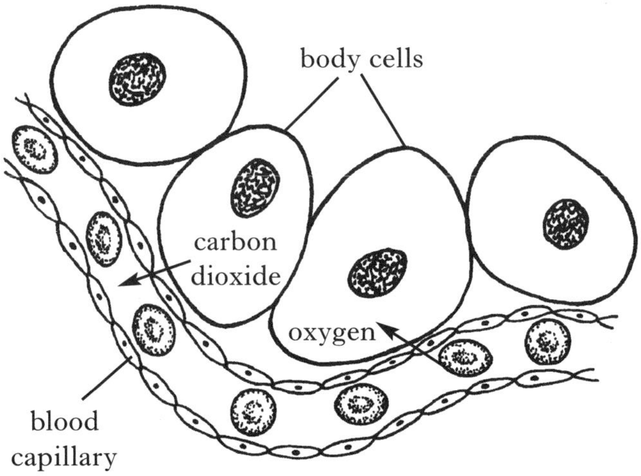


(*a*) Name and describe the process by which carbon dioxide moves out of the body cells into the blood.

Name of process ______________________ **1**

Description of process ______________________________________________

______________________________________________________________ **1**

(*b*) Why is it important that carbon dioxide is removed from the body cells?

______________________________________________________________

______________________________________________________________ **1**

(*c*) Name the cell process which uses oxygen as a raw material.

____________________________ **1**

DO NOT WRITE IN THIS MARGIN

*Marks*

**3.** Three discs were cut from the same potato and were placed in three salt solutions of different concentrations. After 30 minutes the discs were removed from the solutions and the cells examined under a light microscope. A cell from each disc is shown below.

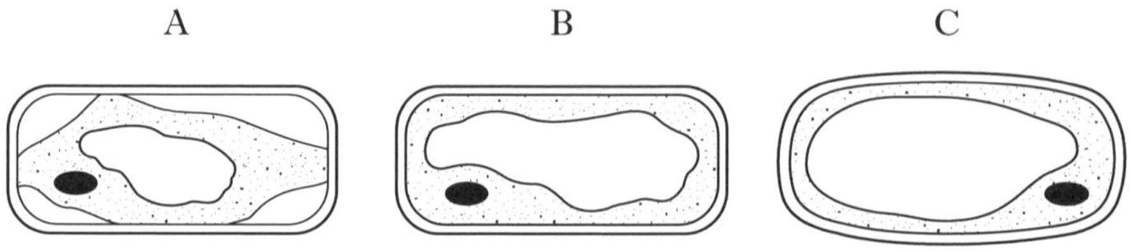


(*a*) (i) Identify the cell which was placed in

a hypertonic solution ____________

an isotonic solution ____________ **1**

(ii) Name the process which causes the difference in appearance of the cells.

______________________________ **1**

(iii) What name is used to describe the condition of cell C?

______________________________ **1**

(*b*) Name the cell structure which prevents plant cells from bursting.

______________________________ **1**

(*c*) Describe the appearance of red blood cells when placed in a hypertonic solution.

______________________________ **1**

(*d*) Name the enzyme which catalyses the synthesis of starch in potato cells.

______________________________ **1**

**[Turn over**

DO I WRIT TH MAR

*Marks*

**4.** (*a*) The corncrake is a bird once found throughout the UK, but now mostly found in the north and west of Scotland.

The decrease in corncrake numbers was caused by a change in hay cutting methods.

Different farming methods were introduced from 1992 to save the corncrake.

The following table shows the estimated numbers of adult corncrake males in Scotland from 1988 to 2001.

| *Year* | *Estimated number of adult males* |
|---|---|
| 1988 | 540 |
| 1990 | 485 |
| 1992 | 440 |
| 1994 | 470 |
| 1996 | 510 |
| 1999 | 590 |
| 2001 | 600 |

(i) Present the results in an appropriate format on the grid below. (Additional graph paper, if required, will be found on page 32.)

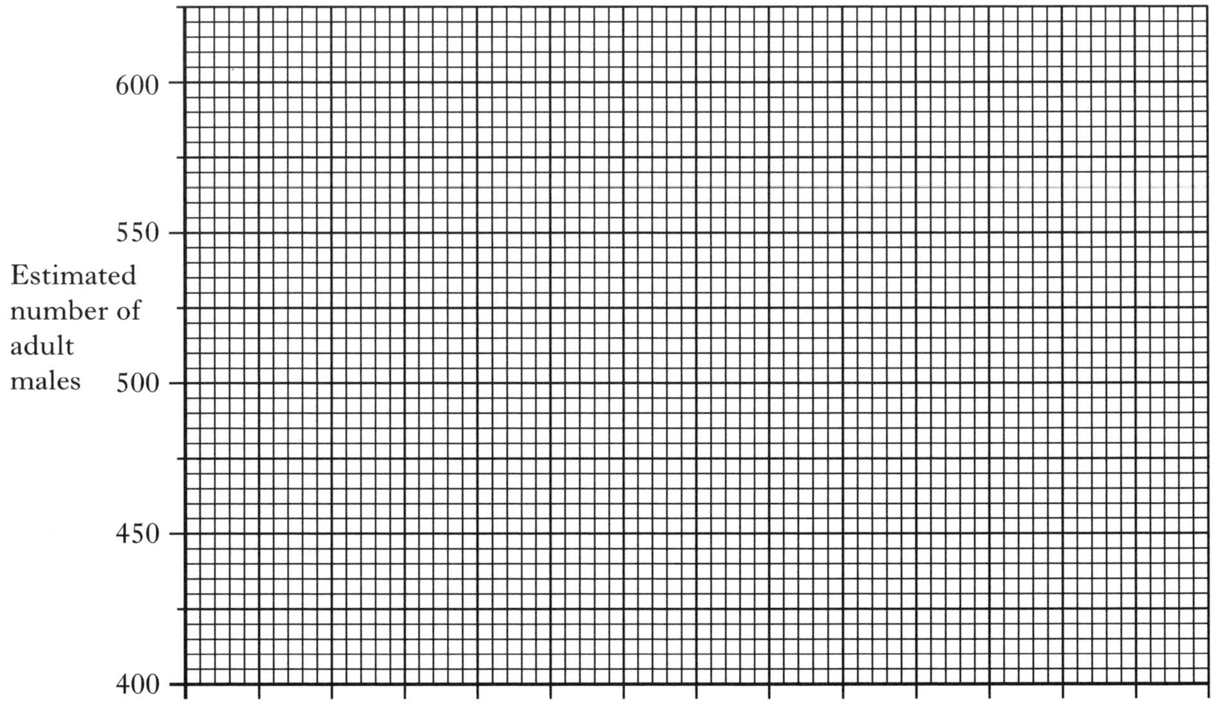


**2**

DO NOT WRITE IN THIS MARGIN

*Marks*

**4. (*a*) (continued)**

(ii) Describe the effect of the introduction of different farming methods on the corncrake population.

____________________________________________

____________________________________________ **1**

(*b*) The change in the corncrake population is the result of human activity. This affects biodiversity.

Give **one** other example of a human activity that affects biodiversity and describe the effect.

Human activity ________________________________ **1**

Effect on biodiversity ______________________________

____________________________________________ **1**

(*c*) The bar chart below illustrates biodiversity in three different meadows.

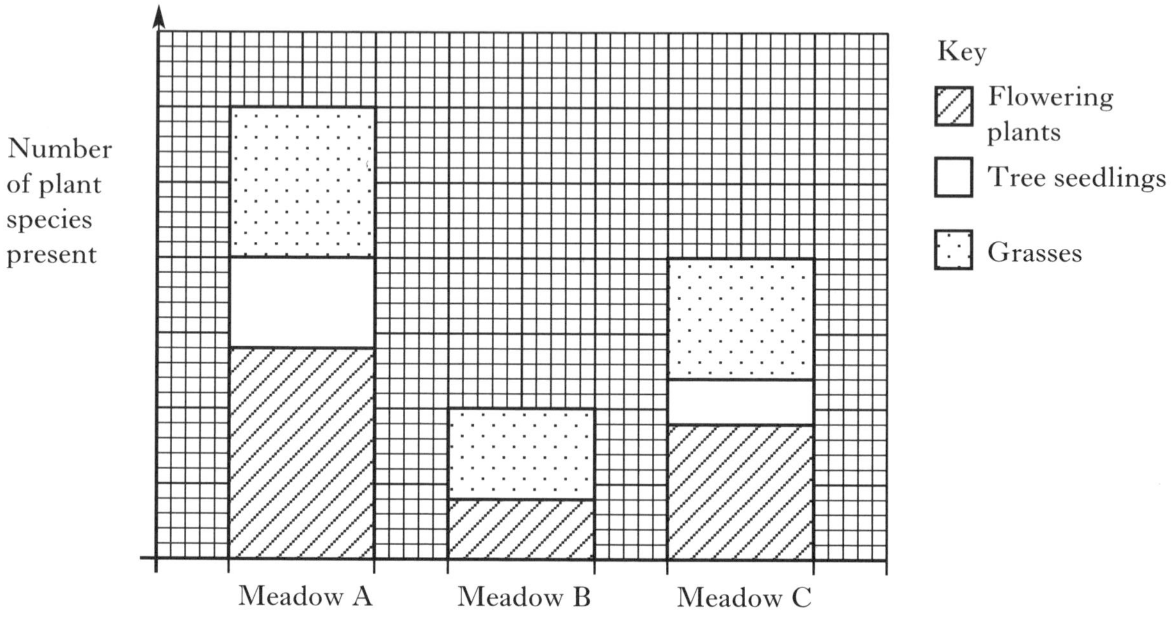


Which meadow has the lowest intensity of grazing?

________________ **1**

(*d*) Describe an adaptation of a desert plant and explain how this adaptation aids survival in desert conditions.

Adaptation ____________________________________ **1**

Explanation ___________________________________

____________________________________________ **1**

Marks

**5.** Brine shrimps are invertebrates that live in salt water. They feed on microscopic green plants filtered from the water.

An investigation into the effect of light on the behaviour of brine shrimps was carried out by five groups of students. The following description and diagram detail how this investigation was set up by each group.

1. A petri dish was half-filled with salt water and six brine shrimps were added.
2. The brine shrimps were allowed to swim around for two minutes.
3. Half of the petri dish was covered in black paper.
4. After a further two minutes the number of brine shrimps found in the light and dark sides was recorded.

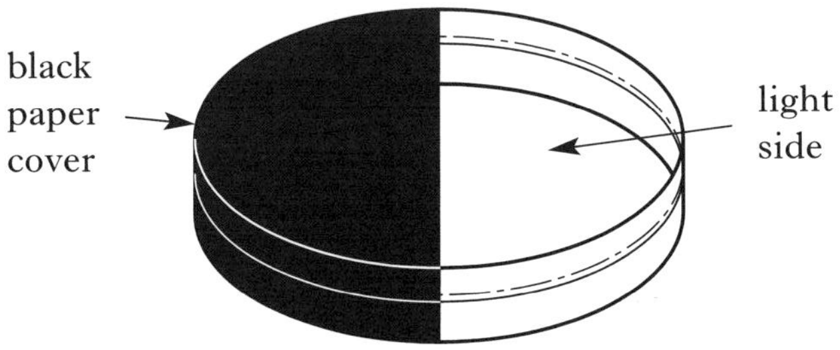


(*a*) State **one** variable that should be kept constant when setting up the investigation.

______________________________ **1**

(*b*) Why were the brine shrimps allowed to swim around for two minutes before the investigation was started?

__________________________________________________________

__________________________________________________________ **1**

DO NOT WRITE IN THIS MARGIN

Marks

**5. (continued)**

(*c*) The results are shown in the table below.

| | *Number of brine shrimps after two minutes* | |
|---|---|---|
| *Student Group* | *Dark side* | *Light side* |
| A | 4 | 2 |
| B | 1 | 5 |
| C | 3 | 3 |
| D | 2 | 4 |
| E | 1 | 5 |
| Total | 11 | 19 |

(i) From the results describe the response of brine shrimps to light.

______________________________________________

______________________________________________ **1**

(ii) Explain why this response helps the brine shrimp survive.

______________________________________________

______________________________________________ **1**

(*d*) Suggest **one** way in which the reliability of the results could be improved.

______________________________________________

______________________________________________ **1**

**[Turn over**

*Marks*

**6.** (*a*) In farmyard fowl, feather type is controlled by a single gene. The allele for normal feathers (N) is **co-dominant** with the allele for extreme frizzle feathers (F) . The results of a cross between two homozygous fowl is shown below.

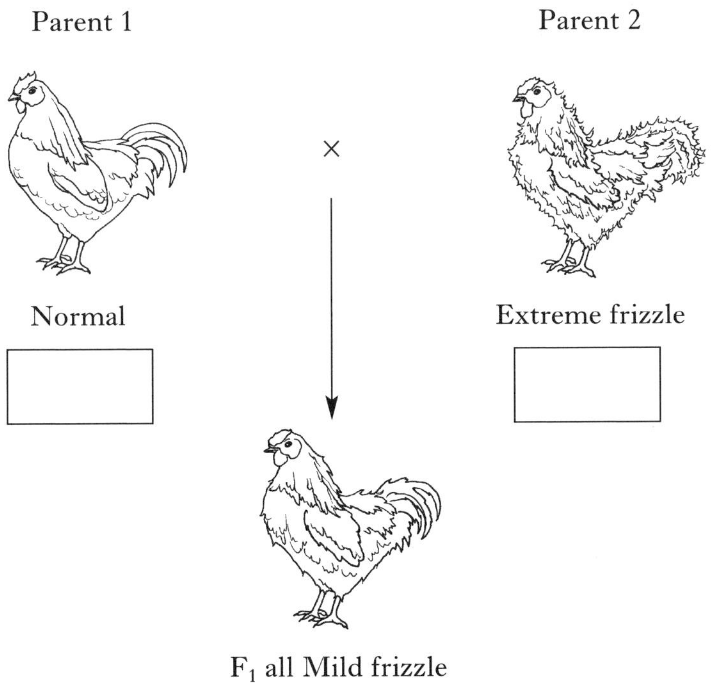


(i) Complete the blank boxes in the diagram above to show the genotypes of the parents. **1**

(ii) Two mild frizzle fowl from the $F_1$ were crossed together.

Complete the punnet square below to show the genotype of the gametes from the $F_1$ male parent and the genotypes of the $F_2$ produced.

| | | genotype of gametes from $F_1$ male parent | |
|---|---|---|---|
| | | | |
| genotype of gametes from $F_1$ female parent | N | | |
| | F | | |

**2**

(iii) State the expected $F_2$ phenotype ratio.

Ratio _____ normal : _____ mild frizzle : _____ extreme frizzle **1**

DO NOT WRITE IN THIS MARGIN

*Marks*

**6. (continued)**

(*b*) Complete the table below by writing the correct word from the list to match the description.

| *List* |
|---|
| interbreeding |
| recessive |
| heterozygous |
| homozygous |
| monohybrid |

| *Description* | *Word* |
|---|---|
| A genotype with different alleles of a particular gene. | |
| An allele which is always masked by a dominant allele. | |
| A type of cross between two true breeding parents that differ in one characteristic. | |

**3**

(*c*) Skin colour is an example of a human characteristic controlled by the alleles of more than one gene.

What name is given to this type of inheritance?

________________________________ **1**

**[Turn over**

DO NOT WRITE IN THIS MARGIN

*Marks*

**7.** The diagram below shows part of a food web found on a rocky shore.

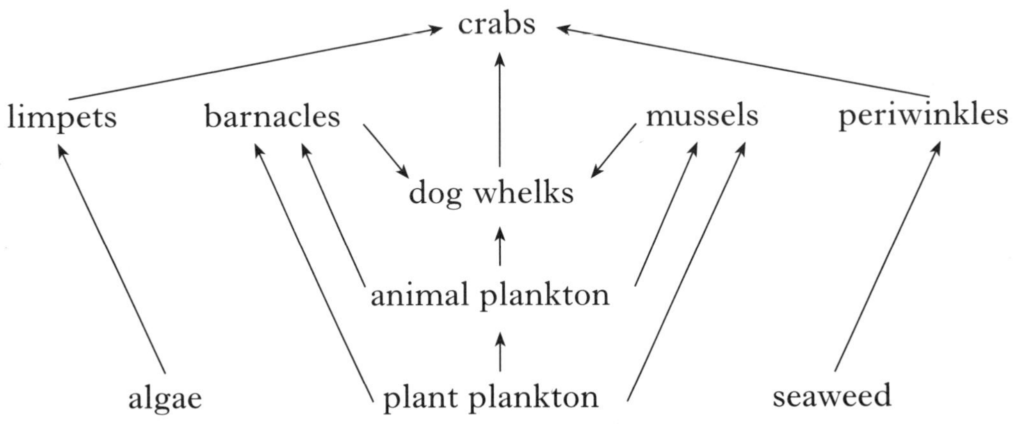


(*a*) Use the words "increases", "decreases", or "stays the same" to suggest what might happen to the populations of barnacles and periwinkles if all the mussels were removed. Give a reason for each answer.

1 Barnacle population ____________________

Reason ____________________

____________________

____________________ **1**

2 Periwinkle population ____________________

Reason ____________________

____________________

____________________ **1**

(*b*) Why is the biomass of algae greater than the biomass of limpets?

____________________

____________________ **1**

*Marks*

**7. (continued)**

(*c*) The following diagram shows a pyramid of energy for part of the rocky shore ecosystem.

The energy values are given in $kJ/m^2/year$.

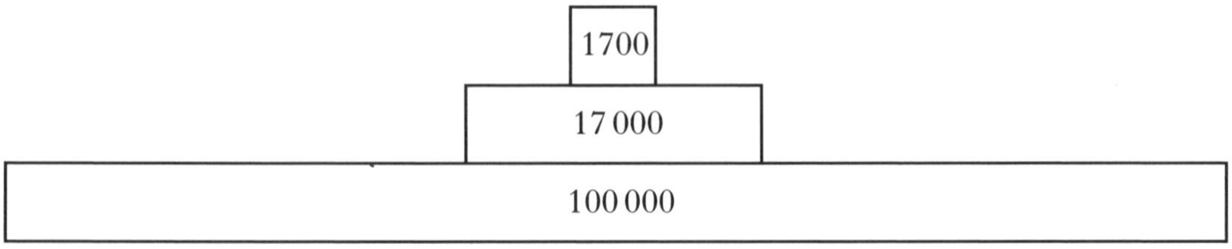


(i) Why does the energy value decrease from one level to the next?

______________________________

______________________________ **1**

(ii) Use information from the food web and the pyramid of energy to complete the table below.

| *Energy value* ($kJ/m^2/year$) | *Niche* | *Named organism* |
|---|---|---|
| 100 000 | | |
| | primary consumer | animal plankton |
| | | dog whelks |

**2**

**[Turn over**

DO NOT WRITE IN THIS MARGIN

*Marks*

**8.** (*a*) The table below gives information about wheat produced by selective breeding over many generations.

| *Generation number* | *Average height of stem* (cm) | *Grain yield (tonnes per hectare)* | *Average length of grain* (mm) |
|---|---|---|---|
| 1 | 142 | 6·0 | 10 |
| 27 | 126 | 6·0 | 9 |
| 45 | 110 | 6·7 | 11 |
| 64 | 106 | 7·5 | 11 |
| 72 | 84 | 8·7 | 10 |

From the table, describe **one** improvement in the wheat and explain why it is a desirable characteristic.

Improvement ________________________________

Explanation ________________________________

________________________________________ **2**

(*b*) Give **one** disadvantage of selective breeding.

________________________________________

________________________________________ **1**

(*c*) Genetic engineering can be used to transfer human genes to bacteria.

(i) Name a human hormone which can be produced by genetically engineered bacteria.

________________________ **1**

DO NOT WRITE IN THIS MARGIN

*Marks*

**8. (*c*) (continued)**

(ii) In the boxes below, describe each of the steps carried out to transfer successfully a human gene to a bacterial cell.

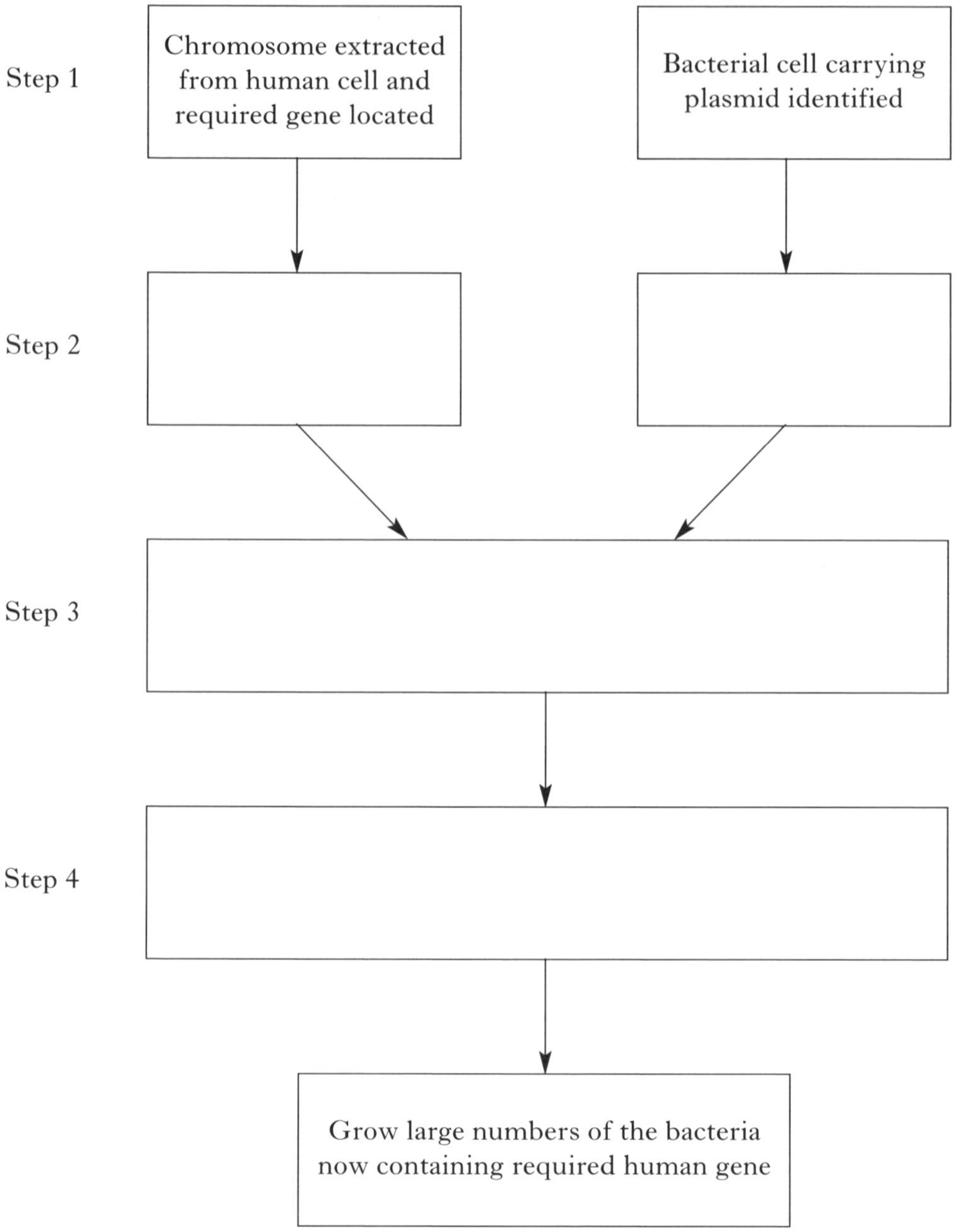


**3**

**[Turn over**

*Marks*

**9.** The diagram below shows the light and dark varieties of the peppered moth, *Biston betularia*.

In an investigation moths were captured in a woodland area, marked and released.

Twenty four hours later moths were recaptured and the results are shown in the table below.

| *Variety* | *Number of moths marked and released* | *Number of marked moths recaptured* | *Percentage recaptured* |
|---|---|---|---|
| Light | 320 | 192 | 60 |
| Dark | 280 | 112 | 40 |

(*a*) (i) Explain why it was necessary to calculate the **percentage** of moths recaptured.

____________________________________________

____________________________________________ **1**

(ii) The results indicate that the investigation was carried out in a non-industrial area.

Explain why the percentage of light coloured moths recaptured is high.

____________________________________________

____________________________________________ **1**

(*b*) What name is given to the process which results in the difference in numbers of these two varieties in this area?

__________________________ **1**

DO NOT WRITE IN THIS MARGIN

*Marks*

**10.** The pulse rate and breathing rate of a student were taken before, during and after a period of exercise. The graph below shows the results obtained.

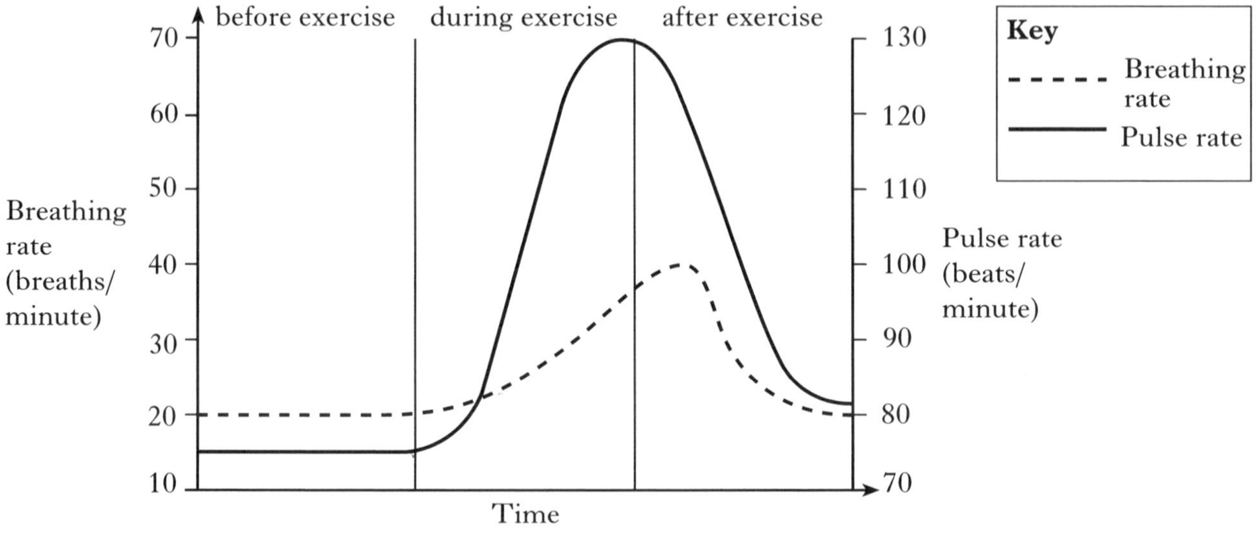


(*a*) (i) Complete the table to show the changes in pulse rate.

| | *Before exercise* | *During exercise* | *After exercise* |
|---|---|---|---|
| *Breathing rate* (breaths/min) | 20 | from 20 to 35 | from 35 to 40 to 20 |
| *Pulse rate* (beats/min) | | | |

**1**

(ii) Explain why breathing rate increases during the exercise.

______________________________

______________________________ **2**

(*b*) Muscle fatigue may occur during exercise. Name the chemical that results in muscle fatigue.

______________________________ **1**

(*c*) (i) Name the structures in the lungs where gas exchange takes place.

______________________________ **1**

[Turn over

DO NOT WRITE IN THIS MARGIN

*Marks*

**10. (*c*) (continued)**

(ii) State **two** ways by which blood carries carbon dioxide around the body.

1 ____________________________________

2 ____________________________________ **2**

(*d*) Underline **one** option in each set of brackets to make the following sentence correct.

In the lungs haemoglobin {combines with / releases} oxygen at {high / low} oxygen levels. **1**

DO NOT WRITE IN THIS MARGIN

*Marks*

**11.** The following diagram shows the human brain.

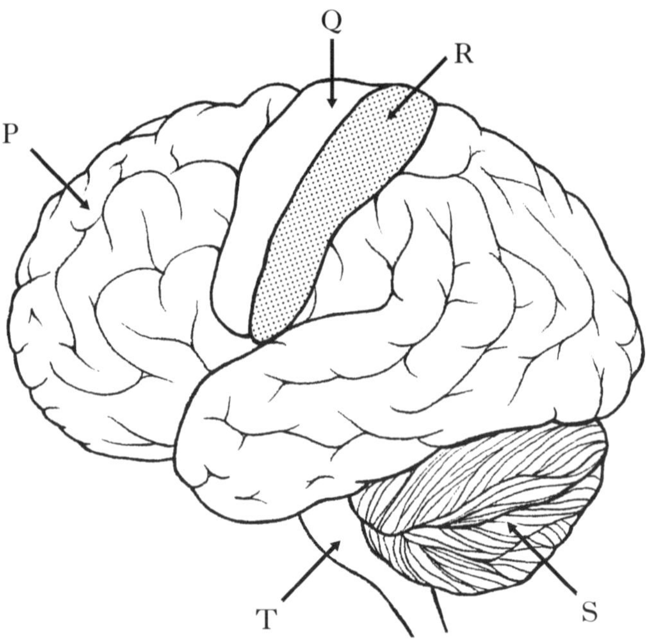


(*a*) Complete the table to identify areas of the brain and their functions.

| *Name of area* | *Letter* | *Function* |
|---|---|---|
| Sensory strip | | Receives nerve impulses from the sense organs |
| Cerebellum | | |
| | T | |

**2**

(*b*) The brain forms one part of the Central Nervous System (CNS).

Name the other part.

______________________________________ **1**

(*c*) Name the type of neurone which links the receptors in the sense organs to the CNS.

______________________________________ **1**

**[Turn over**

DO NOT WRITE IN THIS MARGIN

*Marks*

**11. (continued)**

(*d*) Decide if each of the following statements about temperature regulation in the body is **True** or **False**, and tick (✓) the appropriate box.

If the statement is **False**, write the correct word in the **Correction** box to replace the word underlined in the statement.

| *Statement* | *True* | *False* | *Correction* |
|---|---|---|---|
| External temperature is detected by receptors in the skin. | | | |
| The area of the brain which regulates body temperature is the medulla. | | | |
| Blood vessels in the skin constrict in response to an increase in external temperature. | | | |

**3**

**[Turn over for SECTION C on *Page twenty-eight*]**

## SECTION C

**Both questions in this section should be attempted.**

Note that each question contains a choice.

**Questions 1 and 2 should be attempted on the blank pages which follow.**

**Supplementary sheets, if required, may be obtained from the invigilator.**

*Marks*

**1.** Answer **either** A **or** B.

A. The flow diagram below shows the two stages of photosynthesis.

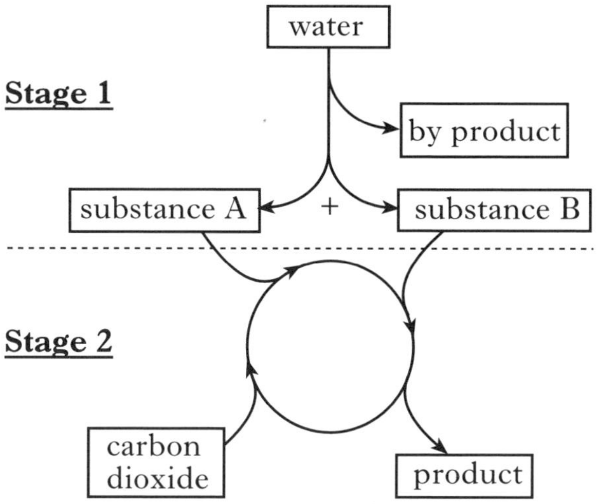


Name and describe **Stage 1** and **Stage 2**. **5**

**OR**

B. The diagram below shows a container used for home wine production.

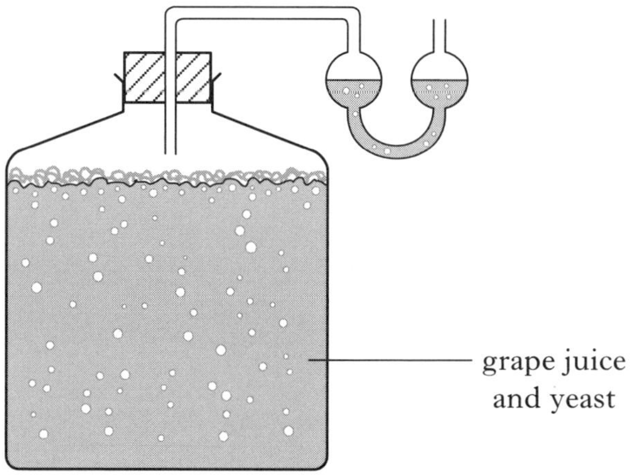


Describe the anaerobic pathway of respiration which results in wine production in this container. **5**

**Question 2 is on *Page thirty*.**

DO NOT WRITE IN THIS MARGIN

*Marks*

**SPACE FOR ANSWER TO QUESTION 1**

*Marks*

**2.** Answer **either** A **or** B.

**Labelled diagrams may be included where appropriate.**

A. Describe the structures of arteries, veins and capillaries. Give the function of each of these types of blood vessel. **5**

**OR**

B. Freshwater bony fish have a water balance problem. State the water balance problem and describe how these fish overcome the problem. **5**

[*END OF QUESTION PAPER*]

DO NOT WRITE IN THIS MARGIN

**SPACE FOR ANSWER TO QUESTION 2**

**SPACE FOR ANSWERS**

ADDITIONAL GRAPH PAPER FOR QUESTION 4(*a*)(i)

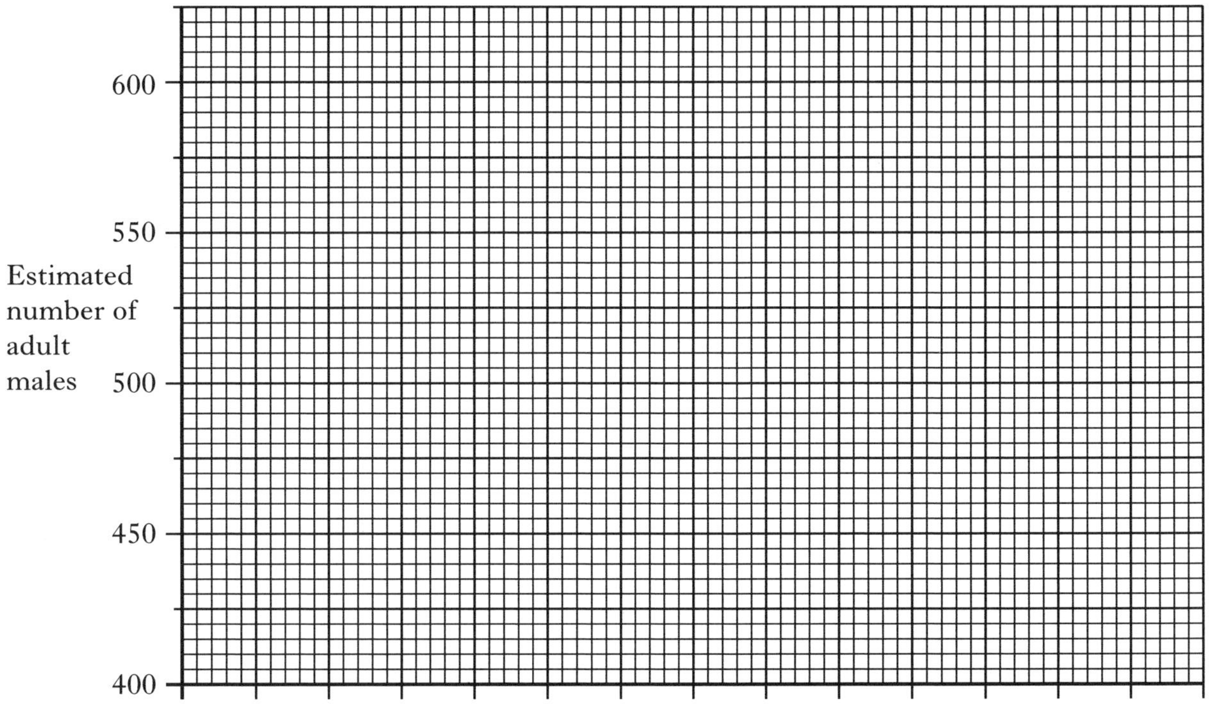